FRONTIERS OF ACCESS TO LIBRARY MATERIALS
No. 6

FRONTIERS OF ACCESS TO LIBRARY MATERIALS

Sheila S. Intner, Series Editor

THE

PRESERVATION PROGRAM BLUEPRINT

Barbra Buckner Higginbotham

Judith W. Wild

AMERICAN LIBRARY ASSOCIATION
Chicago and London
2001

Cover and text design by Dianne M. Rooney

Composition by ALA Editions using Caslon 540 and Caslon 3 typefaces

Printed on 50-pound white offset, a pH-neutral stock, and bound in 10-point Bristol cover stock by McNaughton & Gunn.

The paper used in this publication meets the minimum requirements of American National Standard for Information Sciences—Permanence of Paper for Printed Library Materials, ANSI Z39.48-1992. ∞

Library of Congress Cataloging-in-Publication Data

Higginbotham, Barbra Buckner.
  The preservation program blueprint / Barbra Buckner Higginbotham and Judith W. Wild.
    p. cm. — (Frontiers of access to library materials ; no. 6)
  Includes bibliographical references and index.
  ISBN 0-8389-0802-0
   1. Library materials—Conservation and restoration. 2. Books—Conservation and restoration. I. Wild, Judith W. II. Title. III. Series.

Z701.H54 2001
025.8′4—dc21

00-068959

Printed in the United States of America

05   04   03   02   01   5 4 3 2 1

For
Jayne Poss
and the
Staff of the Hotel Lenado, Aspen, Colorado
There, Many Books Were Written
and for
Martha Wachsman

Contents

Introduction

According to the American Library Association (ALA), some 122,289 libraries of various types exist in the United States—public, academic, school, corporate, medical, law, armed forces, and government.[1] Yet the Association of Research Libraries (ARL) reported only 83 preservation administrators among its 115 members in its 1996–97 report.[2] Although some non-ARL institutions also employ preservation officers, these figures suggest that only a tiny percentage of the libraries in this country include such positions. Another set of numbers, the rolls of the Association for Library Collections and Technical Service's Preservation and Reformatting Section, shows 1,641 members: even if *all* of these were preservation officers, the percentage of libraries employing such persons would still be extremely small—considerably less than 2 percent.

At the same time, every librarian understands that preservation lies at the heart of our most basic trust. From the collections flows everything else that we do—cataloging, reference work, interlending, access. Without library materials (whatever their formats), none of this work would be necessary or even possible. ALA agrees that preservation is an activity that demands the attention of all types of libraries: in its *Preservation Policy*, ALA encourages "all libraries and library professionals to initiate and support preservation efforts at all levels."[3]

Clearly, a great disparity exists between the number of libraries in this country and the number of preservation administrators. Yet librarians and their preeminent professional association acknowledge that every institution should have a preservation program. Notwithstanding the bibliographic equivalent of dividing the fishes and the loaves, how then is this miracle to occur? The answer must be that it is indeed possible for a library to plan and manage a preservation program, although it may not be able to justify a full-time preservation administrator.

The notion that one can run a successful preservation program without a dedicated, on-staff preservation specialist is one ripe for development, because our notion of preservation itself is changing. There has been a clear shift from the item-by-item approach that characterized the '60s, '70s, and '80s to a strategy of addressing entire collections, accompanied by increased emphasis on what the literature calls *preventative* (versus *retrospective*) preservation activity. This newer approach, coupled with a strong interest in the *protective* (versus *curative*) aspects of preservation, emphasizes activities like staff and reader education, emergency planning and recovery, and sound environmental controls.

The Real and the Ideal: Diminishing the Gap

If both individual and organizational interest in preservation has been heightened, and the idea that preservation can be collection- rather than item-based is an accepted one, why doesn't every library in America have a preservation program? Perhaps not every institution has yet gotten the word—to some, preservation may still seem irrelevant ("Why should we have a preservation program? We're not a research library"). But most libraries labor under the impression that a preservation program requires a dedicated preservation officer ("No, we don't have a preservation program. Nobody on our staff has that kind of specialized training"). Put another way, preservation seems out of reach to most libraries that are not part of large or highly specialized institutions ("Our top priority has to be another reference librarian—we can't afford to hire a preservation administrator").

The authors aim here to remove the sort of paralysis vis-à-vis preservation that grips many libraries today by treating preservation as an integral part of the library organization, rather than an independent enterprise. Many authentic needs compete for the human and fiscal resources at the library manager's disposal, and only she or he can fully appreciate and assess the demands and limits of his or her budget. Although not every director can carve out the funds for a preservation officer, this in no way precludes establishing an effective and active preservation program. In short, reproach lies not in the lack of a preservation *specialist* but rather in the absence of a preservation *program*.

This book demonstrates that

- preservation need not be the special province of a handful of research libraries;
- there is economic benefit in implementing a preservation program, and thus all libraries—even those characterized by heavy circulation and a paucity of rare books—can benefit from one;

- a preservation program is within the reach of every library, whatever its size or type;
- planning and administering a preservation program consists of a series of manageable steps; and
- this program will fit neatly into any library's existing organizational scheme.

A Book for All Libraries and All Librarians

This handbook is not confined to the important but restricted audience of preservation specialists. Rather, it is a tool kit for staff working in every functional area of the library, a blueprint for creating and managing a preservation program in any institution. Because preservation is the responsibility of *each* member of the library staff, even the organization lucky enough to have a preservation officer or coordinator will find it impossible to locate every preservation activity in a centralized preservation unit. To ensure and assess the effectiveness of the preservation program, it is critical to delineate each library unit's responsibilities.

This book addresses the needs of all library types—academic, public, school, and special—as well as collections in every format. The premise is that activities necessary to a comprehensive preservation program can be identified, then integrated easily and logically with the general work of one or more library units, whose managers will be responsible for their administration. The good sense of this approach is clear when one considers that the role of the preservation administrator, where such a position exists, is largely one of planning and coordination—it is not the preservation officer who fold-tests paper before a book is cataloged or pulls a ragged binding in the course of reading the shelves. Indeed, it is widely acknowledged that preservation is the responsibility of *every* staff member, in a way that reference service, cataloging, or systems work often is not. Formalizing this responsibility within individual library units is both logical and constructive.

The obvious advantage to identifying those preservation tasks appropriately performed in various library units and incorporating them into these units' routines is that clear *administrative responsibility* for every preservation task is assigned somewhere in the library: staff are not "volunteering" to perform preservation tasks, motivated by their sense of professionalism or love of books. Rather, these activities become part of their duties and routines, so that everyone feels ownership of the preservation program. A preservation team consisting of the heads of each library unit (or their designees) can provide the necessary coordination of activities. (*See* chapter 1, "The Library Director.")

Organizing for Preservation, One Library Unit at a Time

Books about preservation tend to be arranged by such familiar topics as "reader education," "library binding," "environmental controls," and so forth. This works well for preservation specialists but not so well for the thousands of others (reference librarians, catalogers, bibliographers, interlibrary loan staff) who need information about preservation as it relates to their own particular professional focus. So that staff in every department in the library understand their responsibilities (and so they need not sift through pages and pages of material to cull out whatever is of use to them in their own library roles), this book is organized according to the units typically found in many library settings—collection development, circulation, cataloging, access services, and so forth. Those aspects of a preservation program logically performed by staff in such conventional library units are outlined and described in easy-to-follow form. (No single person or unit is responsible for, say, staff education: instead, in this decentralized model, staff education occurs in every unit, tailored for its staff's particular relationship to, and responsibility for, library materials. Similarly, each unit in the library that assists readers integrates public education with its mission and services.[4]) Put another way, this approach is *modular:*

- If a given section does not apply in a particular setting (for instance, suppose a school library outsources its cataloging), that chapter can be easily ignored. It can also furnish points of discussion for the library and the vendor providing the service.

- If a given library unit (building maintenance, for example) does not exist in a particular setting, the responsibilities outlined can be transferred readily to whatever unit (library administration, perhaps) handles those duties.

- If a particular activity occurs in an area of the library other than the one this book suggests, the tasks that are suggested can be easily assigned to that unit.

- If the library is a very small one (there are many one-, two-, or three-person libraries in the United States), perhaps too small to be divided into units, its staff can use this book to identify those preservation activities that will be both beneficial and manageable, and move forward.

Is This the Only Preservation Book You'll Ever Need?

This book ought not eliminate the need for all other preservation reading. This practical manual (whose goal is to inventory and outline preservation activities, showing how each can be integrated with general library operations) should be used in conjunction with the many excellent sources that detail preservation techniques—books that are included in this volume's

"Resource Guide and Bibliography." Rather than discussing *why* binding is important, or describing in detail the many binding techniques available to the modern library, this book shows *where* in a library organization this responsibility might effectively be assigned and outlines the associated duties. Although it includes *curative* approaches (such as repair and binding), the bulk of its advice is squarely centered on the *preventative* aspects of preservation (environmental controls, stack maintenance, processing techniques).

The common though misguided concept that a preservation program demands a preservation officer does nothing to increase the number of preservation programs in American libraries. The approach to preservation that this book takes complements and advances the contemporary view of preservation advocated by the American Library Association.

Notes

1. American Library Association, Library and Research Center, "Fact Sheet Number 1: How Many Libraries Are There in the United States?" [Online], (Chicago: American Library Association, January 2001 [cited 5 January 2001]); available at <http://www.ala.org/library/fact1.html>.

2. Martha Kyrillidou, Michael O'Connor, and Julia C. Blixrud, eds. and comps., *ARL Preservation Statistics, 1996–97: A Compilation of Statistics from the Members of the Association of Research Libraries* (Washington, D.C.: Association of Research Libraries, 1998), xii–xiii. This was the most recent year for which information was available.

3. American Library Association, *Preservation Policy* [Online], (Chicago: American Library Association, 30 June 1991 [cited 5 January 2001]); available at <http://www.ala.org/alcts/publications/preservation.html>.

4. Some libraries may find benefit in centralizing staff and reader education. This book makes provision for that model in chapter 7, "Access Services."

1

The Library Director

Whether or not a library has a preservation officer, the director's responsibility in the preservation program is a substantial one. Without solid administrative commitment and guidance, the preservation program will surely founder.

The library director must spearhead the development of a preservation plan, an agenda for action that will depend entirely upon the library's *purpose* and *collections:* for what reason does this library exist, and what are its collecting goals? The aims of the school or public library with a heavily used circulating collection will differ from those of a historical society or research collection with quantities of older, fragile materials and an explicit mission to support scholarship. Likewise, libraries with substantial nonbook collections (microforms, sound recordings, video formats, electronic media) will have their own distinctive needs. Many libraries will have multiple constituencies, missions, and collections and, consequently, more complex preservation goals. For these reasons, the preservation program must flow from—*complement*—the organization's mission and collection development policy, and it is the director's job to ensure this congruency.

- **Ensure that the library has both a mission statement and collection development policy.**

Put most simply, the library mission statement describes the organization's special purpose or purposes. It should go beyond general statements about those aims to which we all aspire—quality reference service and cataloging—to expressions of the library's distinctive ambitions. The collection development policy follows and reflects the mission statement: here, each institution will identify the subject areas and formats it plans to acquire and support.

1

No "chicken and egg" relationship exists between a library's mission statement and collection development policy and its preservation plan: the former documents *must* come first, and from them the preservation plan and all related choices will then flow. Without these two key statements, neither administration nor staff can know *what* to do in terms of preservation or *why* they are doing it.

- **Appreciate the preservation program as a key aspect of fiscally responsible management.**

Whether the library is one whose stacks are bursting with rare and brittle materials or one in which heavy circulation generates quantities of injured volumes, a preservation program can help address real economic issues. In many instances the library collection is among the parent organization's most valuable capital assets. When one considers the cost per volume of replacing the collection, and adds to that the associated labor costs of selecting, ordering, and processing, a persuasive argument can be made for the sheer fiscal good sense of a sound preservation program. At one midsize publicly funded college, the administration used the worth of the library collection (circa one million volumes) to make its case for a new building. A preservation consultant first assessed the value of the collection and then the longevity of various sections based on paper quality and storage conditions. Next, she projected the added useful life of the collection if it were housed in a new building with quality environmental controls. She demonstrated that, by prolonging the life of the library collections, the state would recoup its multimillion-dollar investment in a new library building in a surprisingly short time. Thanks to her careful investigation, the project was funded.

There are still other ways of looking at the value of a preservation program. Having invested in selecting, ordering, cataloging, processing, housing, and circulating material, libraries must *protect* their investment (and that of the public, the corporation, or other institution who funded this work) by *preserving* it. Furthermore, replacements (and the time spent acquiring and processing them) are costly and detract from funds available to purchase new materials: caring for collections so that this step can be postponed as long as possible is fiscally responsible.

- **Oversee the design of a preservation plan and policy.**[1]

Preservation is a shared responsibility: there is a role for every staff member, and as many staff as practicable should be involved in developing the library's preservation plan and policy. Thus the director will not write the plan him or herself but rather provide leadership for its creation. The preservation plan and policy will include these four elements:

1. *The library's preservation goals and objectives.* The preservation plan will be a sort of action plan, detailing the library's short-term aims, as well as its plans for the future.

2. *A description of the specific preservation activities in which the library will engage.* This part of the plan can be most effectively laid out library unit by library unit:

   • Which preservation responsibilities will be assigned where?

   • What specific activities will be performed to meet these responsibilities?

3. *A statement of preservation priorities, including realistic time frames for achieving each one.* No library can preserve everything—nor should every item be preserved. In this part of the plan, both *activities* (upgrading the building's environmental controls) and specific *collections* (local history archives) will be assigned explicit priorities. Target dates will be attached to each goal. Building surveys (site, environmental, and house-keeping—*see* chapter 2, "The Library Building Manager") and collection condition or needs assessment surveys (*see* chapter 3, "Collection Development and Acquisitions") will generate critical fuel for the library's preservation plan.

4. *The source and type of resources needed to carry out the plan.* These might include

   • staffing,

   • the library's operating budget,

   • new sums the director plans to seek from the administration of the library's parent organization, and

   • projected external funding sources—grants, for example.

• **Provide leadership for changing organizational thinking and culture.**

Introducing a new library program inevitably requires some changes in organizational thinking and culture, and it is the role of the director to provide leadership in several areas. The modular approach this book takes—creating a librarywide preservation partnership by assigning preservation responsibilities within existing units rather than centralizing many of them within a separate preservation department—calls for four steps:

1. *Raise the staff's collective consciousness about the importance of preservation.* A successful preservation program is also a consultative one, involving all library units; this sort of discussion is a good consciousness-raising tool. The director must help staff understand how to *think* about preservation and their own responsibilities within the program. At the same time, she or he should be careful not to present an undertaking whose enormity paralyzes the staff. Indeed, the library may choose to begin simply, as its resources (human, fiscal, spatial) permit. For example, a collection condition survey (with associated cleaning and shelf reading) can be

planned and executed one stack section at a time instead of sending a battalion of workers into the stacks for the sort of full-court press that could be costly for the library and disorienting for readers. Staff must understand that preservation is much more about common sense than it is about chemistry.

2. *Make the staff's preservation responsibilities* explicit *rather than* implicit. In a short time, staff will begin to understand that they are *already* making preservation decisions and doing preservation work—preparing journals for the bindery, keeping the stacks in good order, identifying books that need mending or replacement. But although few staff will be assigned duties that are significantly different from those they are already performing, making preservation responsibilities an explicit part of position descriptions ensures rigor and regularity in performing preservation duties and helps to institutionalize the preservation program. And, because organizations typically *train* staff to perform those tasks assigned to them, establishing explicit preservation responsibilities also ensures a program of staff education.

3. *Build reader education into every staff member's responsibilities.* In terms of changing organizational culture, this is probably the director's most difficult task—but it can also yield rich rewards. Although staff might accept in principle that preservation is everybody's job, almost everyone shrinks from asking a reader to finish his sandwich outside of the building—save that soda for another time and place—or close the covers of books before stacking them atop each other. People do not relish confrontation—it's human nature—and library staff are no exception. Nonetheless, if every staff member, as he or she passed through the library, gently asked readers to observe preservation-related library rules, perhaps with a word of explanation or a gesture to a nearby sign, the impact would be enormous.

4. *Ensure adherence to standards.* There are standards or guidelines that pertain to almost every aspect of preservation, including archivally sound supplies, library binding, and preservation microfilming. The director ensures that each unit manager is familiar with and follows relevant standards.

- **Plan and implement appropriate administrative changes.**

A significant advantage of this modular, integrated approach to preservation is that it should require no major organizational changes. The time the library director might spend establishing smooth and effective interdependencies between a new preservation unit and other library departments can be channeled directly to program support. Nonetheless, the director should expect that a preservation program will call for some degree of resource reallocation, though significantly less than that required to create a new unit by taking staff and funds from various areas. Space issues may arise if the library undertakes new preservation activities (a repair unit, perhaps) that require real estate.

- **Assign responsibility and accountability for preservation.**

Even though no staff member may have the title *preservation librarian, officer,* or *coordinator,* the director will want to assign the overall responsibility for preservation at a high and visible level in the organization. A preservation team (council, committee) reporting to the director and consisting of the library's unit heads, or an enthusiastic representative from each unit, is one approach.

1. *What's in a name?* Does it make a difference what one calls the group whose members are responsible for the implementation, management, and success of the library's preservation program? Yes.

   - *Team* connotes, "We're all in this together and working as equals toward a common goal." Teams typically work together enthusiastically. They get things done. Their energies are marshaled by a team *leader.*
   - *Committee* suggests, "We address democratically issues referred to us." Committees vote. There are lots of them in any organization. Often they wait for assignments.
   - *Council* conveys, "We provide important advice on topics we are presented." Councils are *re*active. They talk and ponder.

   There are roles in libraries for teams, committees, and councils. Whatever the director chooses to call his or her preservation management group, it is to be hoped that its members will function like a team.

2. *Who should serve on the preservation team?* The preservation team will be a powerful group, charged with designing, implementing, and monitoring the preservation program. It may be that the preservation team and the management team are synonymous. (This is one way to ensure that funding and strategic planning for preservation are systematized within the library and that appropriate preservation policies and procedures are included in the procedure manuals for each library unit.) Alternatively, each unit head can appoint a member of his or her staff to the preservation team. This approach will invest preservation responsibility in those staff who are most enthusiastic about the program and thus most likely to work hard for it. It relieves library managers (who may already be overburdened) of yet another responsibility and provides staff development opportunities (along with regular and direct contact with the director) for people from the ranks. Because budget and planning responsibility for each unit still rests with its head, however, considerable collaboration will be needed among director, unit head, and the unit's preservation team member.

• **Provide staff with preservation training opportunities.**

Staff understand that something is important to a director when he or she loosens the library purse strings and spends money for it: there can be no more direct way to communicate enthusiasm for a program than by supporting training for those who must deliver it. A wide range of preservation training opportunities is available in almost every region of the country—everything from library school course work and continuing education classes to workshops and seminars sponsored by local, regional, and national groups. Often such training is highly specific—repair techniques, negotiating a library binding contract, designing a reader education program—making it easy to identify the staff whose attendance could most benefit the preservation program. At a more basic level, if the library offers orientation for new staff, this should contain a preservation element. The sort of general preservation knowledge needed by every staff member can also be added to the library Web site.

• **Bring the preservation message to the library's parent organization.**

Libraries are not independent entities, and each functions as part of a larger organization—a school or university, a corporation, perhaps a city government. Because a preservation program requires resources and other types of support, the library director must ensure that his or her superiors understand the value (both monetary and cultural) of the collections and the corresponding importance of safeguarding them.

• **Influence other key partners.**

The director has natural allies that go beyond the library staff, readers, and the administration of the parent organization. Depending on library type, these partners for preservation can include parents and teachers (school and public libraries), facilities and security staff (any library), and local fire fighting and police forces. Anyone concerned about the costs of libraries and education has the potential to become an effective friend for the preservation program.

• **Negotiate or support cooperative preservation efforts.**

Library consortia can be good sources for training and other preservation services. They may negotiate and make available to members favorable bindery or preservation-microfilming contracts. Where no consortium exists, libraries can form one when they see a benefit to cooperative efforts. The director should support and take advantage of cooperative purchasing power for preservation services, just as he or she does for other library purposes.

• **Budget and obtain funds for preservation.**

Just because the library director opts for a decentralized preservation model and assigns the associated tasks to existing library units does not mean that the preservation program is "free": indeed, it must still be funded and departmental allocations correspondingly increased. If, as part of developing the preservation program, the library significantly increases preservation activities, unit budgets must rise accordingly. For example, a decision to send all new paperbacks to the bindery before they are cataloged and processed would mean an increased allocation for binding.

1. *The preservation plan is the director's blueprint for the preservation budgeting process.* The director will build into existing unit budgets funds for the preservation program—training funds into the staff-development allocation, supplies funds into the budgets of those units that process or repair materials. By adding resources for preservation to each library unit's budget (rather than establishing a separate funding line for the preservation program as a whole) the director is arguably *protecting* the program: in times of fiscal crisis, library managers will look carefully at each established budget area, and the preservation program may well make an easier target than, say, reference service or collection building.

2. *The director acquires the funding necessary for preservation.* Amounts and sources will depend on the library's size, mission, collections, and funding options.

   • The director may seek an increase in the library's general operating budget to support the new preservation program.

   • He or she might also request a series of annual and nonrecurring supplements to the budget for particular projects—equipment for a repair center or binding that has been allowed to accumulate and too long deferred. Gift funds also make good sources of support.

   • Unrestricted gifts can easily be put to use, and it should not be hard to convince donors that their support can be used as logically to *preserve* what the library already owns as it can be to *increase* the size of the existing collections.

   • When the library accepts the gift of a new collection (particularly if the materials it contains are in need of treatment), the director may ask the donor to provide either an endowment to address the collection's ongoing conservation needs or an outright grant for this purpose. It is not uncommon for donors to support both collection condition surveys and the treatments that the survey results suggest.

   • Grants can be a solid source of support for the preservation program. State agencies and private foundations may provide funding for collection condition or needs assessment surveys. Once a survey indicates the library's principal preservation needs (for instance, rehousing archival collections that support an important local history program), additional resources may be available to support this work. The director may assume the responsibility for preservation grant writing and management, or the preservation team may delegate this work, according to the purpose of the grant.

- When another institution requests the loan of a title that is not in the pink of health, the library can agree to lend with the proviso that the borrowing organization fund the needed treatment. Admittedly, this is a very slow path to preserving the collection, yet it will address the needs of what can be some of the library's more popular items.

- **Administer space in a preservation-conscious fashion.**

Library managers govern the allocation of three primary resources—dollars, personnel, and space. It is readily apparent how choices about funding and staffing affect a preservation program, but decisions about how space will be used are equally important.

- Is the building laid out so that shelves are removed from strong sources of heat and light (windows, skylights, atria)?
- Are storage areas distant from sources of water, steam, and damp?
- Is shelving laid out so that it is removed from exterior walls?
- Is there enough shelving so that items sit comfortably (rather than jam-packed) on shelves?

If the answer to any of these questions is no, the director may opt to reduce, relocate, or compress other library functions to make way for shelving or perhaps install compact stacks. Ultimately, the director may need to plan for an expansion of the library building, or a new building, when factors like environmental controls are also creating preservation problems. (For more on this topic, *see* chapter 2, "The Library Building Manager.")

- **Build the preservation program into every construction project.**

The director works closely with architects to ensure that the design of new construction supports the preservation program.

1. *Build in defenses against fire, flood, and quake.* Here, decisions related to design, site, and construction will have important impacts.

2. *Include lighting whose type and location are consistent with preservation goals.*

3. *Provide for suitable environmental controls.* Comprehensive top-of-the-line environmental controls can easily cost more than almost any other aspect of a library building project. Mechanical systems that one can calibrate precisely enough to maintain temperature and relative humidity at desirable and constant levels are expensive both to *purchase* and to *operate*. In many building projects, compromises will be necessary: "the best" is costly, and most project budgets are finite. In the end, the level of control may differ from area to area in the building, with special collections or the archives receiving a more finely calibrated system than does the general collection.

4. *Allow for a security or theft detection system.*

5. *Make use of a preservation consultant.* On any major construction project, there will be a raft of consultants: perhaps one of these should be a preservation consultant, particularly if the collections are exceedingly fragile, have significant value (monetary, cultural, scholarly), or have been exposed to water or mold in the past and are thus especially vulnerable to reinfection. Although the cost may not be small, the advice of a competent preservation consultant during the design phase of a new building project has the potential to generate real savings down the road.

- **Guide the development of an emergency preparedness and recovery plan.**[2]

Although quaint and reassuring, the old adage, "Don't borrow trouble. If trouble is going to come, it will come soon enough," serves no library well when it comes to disaster preparedness. Better to adopt the Girl Scout motto and "Be prepared," because solid preplanning is the easiest way to survive a disaster and ensure a smooth recovery. The following eight steps are some that directors should take.

1. *Establish the value of the collections.* The library collection is a proud but vulnerable treasure. As suggested earlier in this chapter, if one multiplies the number of volumes in the library by, say, $100 (probably a conservative figure when the several costs associated with replacement—reordering, cataloging, processing—are added to the actual price of a new volume), it is easy to see that the collections may well outvalue the building that shelters them. It is important that the director help the organization the library serves to see that recovery plans are well worth the money, especially when considered in the context of what could well be a multimillion-dollar asset.

2. *Develop a budget for the disaster preparedness and recovery planning process.* The emergency planning process itself requires both money and staff time. The director will allocate funds to design and test an emergency preparedness and recovery plan and train library and other campus staff in their associated duties.

3. *Provide leadership for identifying and implementing a series of relevant preventive measures.* Disaster *prevention* is an important component of planning for disaster *response*, and slighting preventative measures can increase the amount of damage and loss that occurs during an emergency. The director (or the building manager, where such a position exists) will work with the parent organization's facilities management staff to identify building problems and then develop a plan for correcting them before they lead to disaster. (The plan might include such things as repairing or replacing leaking windows and roofs, installing

water detectors, and regularly inspecting fire alarms and smoke detectors.) Similarly, the library manager and the head of security can design a plan for enhancing the safety of the collections. Some of the elements in such a document might be schedules for the regular recertification of fire extinguishers and conducting fire drills.

4. *Provide direction for producing a disaster preparedness and recovery plan.* A detailed and written plan will save the lives of many library materials when disaster strikes and confusion reigns. One of the first steps the director must take is to assemble an emergency planning team—professionals and supporting staff selected from various areas of the library who will develop a disaster preparedness and response plan. The library manager will also enlist the participation of security, physical plant, and maintenance staff (some of those "key partners" mentioned earlier in this chapter), giving these units a sense of ownership in the library's emergency preparedness program. He or she should ensure that the plan

   - prioritizes collections for recovery;
   - addresses the needs of the many types of materials the library may contain (paper, film, electronic formats); and
   - includes the safety of staff, readers, and equipment.

5. *Decide to whom to delegate authority during an emergency.* The director must establish an emergency chain of command and determine who will assume authority when an emergency occurs. Reliability and strong leadership skills are essential qualities for all members of the disaster response team but especially for its leaders. Here, the director may select the library's building manager (where such a position exists), or a person who has proven him- or herself in another emergency situation, or a staff member who has actually engaged in disaster recovery. For many reasons, appointing a *pair* of recovery team leaders is a good idea:

   - There will be a great deal of work for only one person to accomplish.
   - If there are two team leaders, their schedules can be arranged so that one of them is generally present.
   - A team of two can be chosen from different library units, so that no one program is seriously disadvantaged.

   The director must let the library staff know that the team leaders have been given full authority when disaster strikes: in an emergency, they are empowered to reassign staff from any area of the library to recovery work.

6. *Seek qualified external guidance and assistance.* The director may invite police officers and firefighters to tour the building, familiarizing them with the disaster response plan and building layout. Seeking the help of a consultant in writing the emergency plan or training staff in recovery procedures can also be a sound investment; a qualified preservation pro-

fessional who is already familiar with the building, staff, and collections may prove invaluable *when* (not *if*) disaster strikes. There are library and archival organizations, consortia, and associations that provide preservation education, information, and training; the director may wish to contact them.[3]

7. *Identify sources of funds for cleaning up, recovering, and replacing lost collections.* Disasters are costly events; weddings and bar mitzvahs pale beside them. Despite the fact that recovering, drying, and reshelving the collections may be less expensive than replacing them, the director must still identify resources for this work. Many publicly funded institutions are "self-insured," a euphemism for "uninsured." However, if the parent organization has insurance, the director should be certain that she or he understands both the coverage and the company. The library manager should meet with the parent institution's risk manager and insurer to determine what insurance covers, where limitations lie, and how much money can be expended before the insurance company arrives on the scene. If the institution is uninsured or has a high deductible, the director must determine whether a local contingency fund of some sort exists and who has the authority to allocate emergency funding. Determining the value and replacement costs of all assets, including books, furniture, equipment, and nonprint collections, will help the library manager justify insurance coverage or access to emergency funding.

8. *Establish appropriate relationships and routines with other divisions of the parent organization (facilities management, security, human resources, food services, etc.).* It is important that the director predetermines the type and extent of assistance the library can expect from physical plant, maintenance, and security staff during a disaster, then establish appropriate emergency routines.

   - It is a good idea to include security, maintenance, and physical plant staff in emergency planning sessions that are relevant to their roles.
   - The library manager must also discuss with the parent organization's labor relations specialist reassigning staff to the sort of work that emergencies often necessitate; this can speed the recovery process and help eliminate concerns about "working out of title" (that is, taking on responsibilities outside one's job description) when a disaster actually occurs.
   - The director will also talk with the institution's food services operation about the possibility of using freezers as safe, temporary, time-buying solutions. (In an academic setting, the disaster's timing can mean everything: during intercession or holiday periods, large

amounts of cafeteria freezer space may be available. When school is in session, the library will probably have to look elsewhere.)

- **Provide leadership during emergency recovery.**

Recovery is a lengthy process. Months, perhaps more than a year, may pass before a building completely dries out or damaged collections are returned from outside treatment facilities and reprocessed. Moreover, once a building has experienced a water-based emergency, it is often left more vulnerable to certain predators, such as mold and fungi. Unfortunately, disasters are not necessarily "one to a customer." In fact, after the first, most pressing issues have been addressed—the floors have been wet-vac-ed, the books are drying, and replacement and retention decisions are being made—the real work begins. Here are some of the library director's responsibilities, après emergency:

1. *Obtain commitments for funds, repairs, and other needed resources from the parent organization's administration or trustees.* Purchasing materials to replace destroyed collections is just one cost center in disaster recovery. The fees of companies that freeze, dry, and remove mold from damaged volumes; the costs associated with reordering and processing new materials; the staff time required to repatriate and reprocess treated books— all these costs are both real and substantial. And perhaps more than just the collections has been affected by the emergency: the building may require costly repairs as floor tiles come up, ceiling tiles come down, and plaster buckles. Furniture can be ruined. Expensive computer equipment may be destroyed. A major task for the library director will be securing the funds needed for complete recovery.

2. *Acknowledge the efforts of the staff.* While the response team manages the immediate rescue work, the director should be visible and interested in the actions and needs of the library staff. It is the director who must maintain the momentum during disaster recovery by making key management decisions and working with library boards or administrations. The library director should commend (orally and in writing) the disaster team leaders and other staff who were key in the recovery effort, recognizing the value of their contributions. Similar recognition from key members of the parent organization's administration will also make the staff feel that their hard work is appreciated.

3. *Communicate a set of reasonable expectations for library staff to the administration or trustees of the parent organization.* This is one of the director's most important responsibilities. It is a mistake to discount the amount of unpleasant physical labor involved in dealing with an emergency: working in rancid water; pulling hundreds of wet books off shelves and loading them onto trucks or wrapping and boxing them; wet-vac-ing floors; handling reeking, fungi-infested books while wearing gloves and

masks—none of these tasks is easy or pleasurable. Furthermore, *this type of work is in no one's job description,* and an organization should count itself lucky when the staff rises to the occasion following an unfortunate event. An expectation on the part of the board of trustees or the parent organization's administration that library staff will work long hours stoically and without complaint (or even *with complaint*), out of title and under the most unpleasant physical circumstances, is unrealistic and unfair. It is the responsibility of the library director to help the administration or trustees understand not only that the staff's efforts are worthy of remark, but that extra labor may be necessary when the emergency is very severe. Under some circumstances, kind words and party cakes may be insufficient palliatives.

4. *Establish new or temporary staffing patterns.* Following an emergency, some temporary job reassignments may be necessary. The director may also authorize additional working hours for some staff or hire temporary employees to get displaced materials reshelved or new materials ordered, processed, and cataloged.

5. *Work with consultants and vendors who are brought in to assist in the recovery process.* When the emergency is especially serious or far-reaching, the help of consultants or companies that provide recovery services (such as drying out either collections or buildings) may be indicated. The director will select appropriate assistance and monitor the work performed.

6. *Interact with the media.* If the disaster is a major one—significant fire or earthquake damage, for example—local journalists and newscasters may be on the doorstep. The director (perhaps assisted by the parent organization's public relations officer) will interact with members of the press to ensure that the event is accurately reported.

7. *Put the building back together.* This may be no small matter. Decisions about replacing furniture, equipment, and critical library systems will present themselves. Staff work spaces, administrative offices, and their functions are often overlooked in disaster response; however, at the same time the library confronts collection damage, the staff may also face disaster very close at hand, their desks filled with water, paper documents fused together in clumps, waterlogged computers that once housed the digital originals. These problems will also demand the director's attention.

8. *Evaluate the library's response to the emergency and adjust the recovery plan appropriately.* While recovery is in full swing, it is the job of the emergency response team to keep track of problems that deserve review when the crisis is over. The director, assisted by the team, will reexamine these issues postdisaster and modify the plan as experience suggests.

9. *Develop disaster documentation.* Whether the library is insured or not, the director must see to it that the event is thoroughly documented—from the very beginning when it was discovered and through the initial recovery process and the steps required for complete recovery. This report must also include the costs associated with recovery: staff time, supplies and other materials, building repairs, and the fees charged by companies that clean, dry, freeze, or repair damaged collections. (Photographic documentation is also highly effective.) The report may be tailored to a particular audience—the board of trustees, the parent organization's administration—or written more generally, for use with a variety of constituencies. The information contained in such a document can help to prevent another disaster or to effect needed improvements in the library facility. Suddenly, the library may move to the top of the list of local renovation projects.

10. *Determine when to reopen the library or resume the delivery of services.* Sometimes, this decision is an obvious one: if the emergency is limited to certain areas of the building, these may be closed to the public during the recovery process while the rest of the building and its service points remain open. On the other hand, an accident like the one in which concrete dust was distributed throughout an entire building, or one in which building safety is in question following a natural disaster, requires greater analysis and external consultation before a decision to reopen the building or resume library service can be made.

11. *Initiate a fund-raising campaign.* If the disaster has been a major one and the financial implications are large, the library director should consider initiating a fund-raising effort as soon as the immediate response period is ended. For maximum effectiveness, the campaign should begin shortly after the disaster's occurrence.

12. *Let other institutions know that the director and the staff will be there for them, should disaster strike.* A library that has managed and recovered from an emergency can be a great deal of help when another institution faces a similar crisis.

• Select preservation consulting assistance.

Once, we did not go to the doctor unless we felt sick. But today most people have a more enlightened view of health care: they practice *preventive* medicine, making appointments for regular checkups, flu shots, and so forth. Everyone has a personal physician, although any one doctor serves as personal physician to many people.

This medical analogy makes a lot of sense for the care of a library's collection: instead of a library's having a full-time preservation officer on staff and dedicated to its materials alone, the director can choose to have a "personal preservation librarian" to whom she or he turns for preventive care, as well as help when emergency strikes. The library manager can take these steps:

1. *Calculate the cost of using a preservation consultant.* Consulting fees and related costs (food, accommodation, travel) vary considerably from place to place, but by making a few telephone calls to local or regional preservation service centers, the director can determine what it will take to hire a preservation consultant on an hourly or daily basis. With some simple math, the director can make a sound case for this approach. If a consultant can be hired at the rate of $400 a day, three weeks of time would cost $6,000 (plus reimbursables)—and a great deal can be accomplished in three weeks. The director might also consider offering a retainer, guaranteeing the consultant so many days of work each year, rather than entering into a simple call-as-need-be agreement. This approach could net a more favorable daily rate.

2. *Plan the budget for preservation consulting.* The director should consider how much the library's budget will bear and what his or her top priorities for this specialist might be, then budget for so many days when preparing the next year's financial plan. A comparison of the salary for a full-time librarian (say, $40,000 plus 20 percent for benefits) with the amount proposed for preservation consulting should make a persuasive case for this approach. The director can point out that the parent institution is spared the cost of providing costly benefits like health insurance and retirement plans when it uses consulting help. And if disaster strikes, the director may well be able to charge the associated consulting costs somewhere other than the library budget: when a contractor's negligence causes an emergency, his insurer may pay the preservation consultant's expenses and fees but decline to cover the cost of library staff time devoted to recovery. In such cases, the organization will be financially better off with a consultant.

3. *Consider affiliating with a preservation service center rather than a particular consultant.* An organization like the Northeast Document Conservation Center (NEDCC) provides training, conservation treatment, and an array of additional preservation services. In fact, NEDCC's purpose is to provide conservation services to libraries that do not have in-house conservation staff and laboratories or those with limited facilities. The library director should know what local or regional centers are available and the services each offers. It is important to understand that some areas of the country are blessed with such support—in the Northeast exist both NEDCC (Andover, Massachusetts) and the Center for Art and Historic Artifacts (Philadelphia). In other parts of the country, however, such services may not exist.

4. *Identify suitable consultants.* Getting reliable recommendations will not be difficult.

- Many library and archival organizations, consortia, and associations maintain consultant rosters that include names, education and other qualifications, and areas of expertise. (Some of these organizations provide preservation education, information, and training themselves— the director will want to inquire.)

- If there are nearby research libraries, their preservation officers may be able to recommend other avenues or even specific names.

- There can be decided advantages to working with a consultant who is relatively local. This will save the library the cost of airfare and other transportation expenses, as well as long-distance telephone and fax bills. More importantly, in the event of an emergency the preservation specialist will be able to respond quickly. On the other hand, a particular specialist's breadth of experience, abilities, and flexibility may make the cost of a long-distance relationship well worthwhile.

- A word of caution: some preservationists with full-time jobs also consult. Of necessity, their time and availability are less flexible than those of someone who consults for a living. (If on Monday morning the stacks are flooded, the director will want someone who can react speedily.) Even with full-time consultants, however, there are no guarantees: following a widespread disaster like Hurricane Andrew, almost every preservation consultant in the country was busily employed in the Sunshine State, and hiring consulting help was almost impossible.

5. *Determine the characteristics the preservation consultant should possess.* How specialized or general should a consultant's training be? The list of activities under number 6, below, suggests that it may not be easy to find someone who can be all things to one's library. In choosing a consultant, the director might take the following steps:

- Ask questions: review the sorts of things that need to be done, whether this year or next, and assess a consultant's abilities in each area.

- Talk to references.

- Just as people see medical authorities when the need arises, call in someone with particular expertise in unusual circumstances.

6. *Identify an array of tasks for the preservation consultant.* A qualified preservation consultant can help any library staff accomplish these basic tasks.

- Prepare an emergency response manual. Writing an emergency plan and training staff in recovery procedures are arguably more important for libraries that lack resident preservation expertise than for those that have it. When disaster strikes, a qualified consultant who is already familiar with the building, the staff, and the collections will have a running start.

- Conduct staff training. Disaster recovery is only one field for staff training. Stack maintenance is another key area. Moreover, cataloging and collection development staff should be taught how to recognize materials (including gifts) in need of preprocessing preservation treatment.

- Develop a plan for correcting building problems. Assessing the library building and addressing problems before they lead to disaster is a worthwhile project. Such a plan might include repairing or replacing leaking windows and roofs, installing water detectors, regularly inspecting fire alarms and smoke detectors, and so forth.

- Prepare a collection retention plan. Establishing retention and discard priorities for each major collection (in advance of an emergency!) and creating floor plans showing where these collections are located is a must for any library. The preservation specialist can work with bibliographers (whose emotional ties to the collections they've developed will be much greater than the consultant's) so that decisions can be made efficiently and economically, should the need arise.

- Provide leadership for disaster recovery. When emergencies occur, it is almost impossible to overstate the value of assistance from a knowledgeable professional who can organize the staff and supervise the rescue effort. The consultant can also assess the degree of damage and recommend longer-term recovery procedures. Written reports can prove very useful: often an expert's recommendations can win the attention of the library board or other top administrators.

- Conduct collection condition surveys. Every library has certain collections it considers to be of significant monetary or cultural value (in our setting, incunabula have monetary value, and our Brooklyniana collection has cultural importance). Carrying out collection condition surveys of such collections, perhaps in advance of seeking grant funds to perform the preservation work the survey will suggest, is an excellent project.

- Develop grant proposals. Many agencies fund preservation projects, and a specialist with the proper expertise can prepare competitive proposals. A consultant can work with the staff who have developed targeted collections to write grant applications aimed at improving their condition. Some agencies also fund preservation needs assessments, a useful starting point for any library. A good consultant will be aware of the grant opportunities that are available.

- Carry out various special projects. A preservation consultant can be of great help with library renovation or expansion projects. The study mentioned earlier in this chapter—the one that resulted in funding for a new library—was conducted by a consultant. The new building is a multimillion-dollar project, so it seems safe to say that the money invested in the consultant was well spent. A preservation specialist can also advise on environmental controls for a new building, how best to protect the collections during construction, or any number of additional topics.

Retaining a consultant as the library's preservation specialist is a valuable idea, if for no other reason than (to paraphrase a rather rude expression) "Disasters happen." When it comes to emergencies, it's much better to be an ant than a grasshopper: every library should prepare for a future that will almost certainly include one or more disasters.

- **Ensure that the preservation program has a strong assessment component.**

No plan or program stands still: like every other library initiative, the preservation program is dynamic and deserves periodic review if it is to remain effective and vital. This assessment should include, and might start with, the emergency preparedness and recovery plan.

Notes

1. Many books offer guidance in developing a preservation plan, and several are referenced in this book's "Resource Guide and Bibliography." Among the better resources is the Northeast Document Conservation Center's *Preservation of Library and Archival Materials: A Manual,* 3d ed., rev. and expanded [Online], ed. Sherelyn Ogden (Andover, Mass.: Northeast Document Conservation Center, 1999 [cited 5 January 2001]); available at <http://www.nedcc.org/plam3/newman.htm>.

2. Karen E. Brown, *Worksheet for Outlining a Disaster Plan* [Online], (Andover, Mass.: Northeast Document Conservation Center, 1999 [cited 5 January 2001]); available at <http://www.nedcc.org/plam3/tleaf34.htm>.

3. *See* the "Resource Guide and Bibliography" that follows chapter 12. Many of these groups either provide consulting services or can recommend consultants.

2

The Library
Building Manager

The library building is the collection's most fundamental source of security, its first line of defense. For this reason, its mechanical systems, maintenance, and other protective qualities are key to the preservation mission.[1] This means that the job of the library building manager is among the most important in the preservation program.

Not every library will have a building manager—not every library occupies an entire building. Where the library (corporate or school, for example) is one of several tenants, a building manager will likely report to whomever "owns" the building—the school principal or (in a corporate or academic setting) the head of a facilities management unit. In such cases, some of the duties outlined for the library building manager may fall to the library director or another member of the administrative team. Alternatively, and depending on the director's interpersonal skills and talents of persuasion, he or she may succeed in establishing many of the tasks outlined below as part of the responsibilities of a larger facilities management unit, even though no reporting relationship exists.

- **Establish a collaborative relationship with the facilities management unit.**

Few libraries are independent entities; instead, almost every library serves and is part of a larger parent organization—a school, a city, a college, a corporation. For this reason, whether or not the library has its own building manager (as larger libraries often do), its parent organization is sure to have a facilities management unit whose cooperation and goodwill are essential to the library's success in any number of areas. These are the people who repair that broken pipe, then replace the wet carpet and repair the walls.

They may also control the library's heating, air-conditioning, and other mechanical systems, and they are often the first to discover an emergency—the flood or fire that begins after the library closes for the day. (This is why the building manager provides library floor plans to the facilities management unit, as well as local fire and police departments.)

Preservationist Nancy Gwinn urges that the library's administrative staff work hard at understanding the facilities management unit's constraints and problems—that the library building manager partner with them to address the many limitations and frustrations that older (or poorly constructed) buildings and their systems often present. Facilities management staff will have many clients besides the library, so that styling oneself as an empathetic comrade in arms, instead of a ceaseless nag, is a sound strategy. Like the library, facilities management will have its own resource issues as it attempts to stretch available dollars and staff to meet the needs of every building and space for which it is responsible. The library building manager's willingness to cooperate and compromise can be key to achieving the best possible outcomes for the collections, staff, and readers.[2]

- **Know the history of the library building.**

Many people are unaware that a building's history has considerable capacity to effect its future. Knowledge of the disasters of times past equips the building manager to prevent or control those of the present and future.

- The flood caused by an eroded seal on a steam valve has the very real possibility of recurring, unless repairs were subsequently done on all remaining valves.

- Once a building has experienced water damage, lingering mold spores can make it far more vulnerable to reinfection, should the humidity rise dramatically.

- **Schedule and conduct a series of building surveys.[3]**

The building manager schedules and conducts at least three different types of building surveys: site, environmental, and housekeeping. After analyzing the results, he or she then develops a plan for correcting the problems that are identified.

1. *The site survey.* The building survey is the starting point for developing the library's emergency preparedness and recovery plan mentioned in chapter 1, "The Library Director." It will reveal weaknesses that must be corrected if the building is properly to play its protective role. The library building manager—working with facilities management staff, the insurance company, the local fire department, and others as need be—inventories building problems (leaking windows and roofs, the absence of fire alarms or smoke detectors) and takes steps to address them. If the library is housed in an architecturally important building, its integrity must also be taken into account.

2. *The environmental survey.* A sound environment is widely acknowledged as fundamental to an effective preservation program. The environmental survey will reveal whether temperature, relative humidity, and filtration systems are regulated so that they deliver the best possible environment for collections that are coexistent with staff and readers. Does air move freely throughout the building, preventing pockets of humidity (and the mold that can follow) from developing? Most funding agencies will not support a preservation project unless a library demonstrates (perhaps via an environmental survey) that it is able to provide a suitable climate for the collections the grant request addresses.

3. *The housekeeping survey.* Keeping the library free of dust and dirt is another aspect of the preservation program. The housekeeping or custodial survey will identify steps (regular trash removal, increasing the number of wastebaskets, a dusting program) that will lead to cleaner collections.

- **Monitor the heating, ventilation, and air-conditioning systems (HVAC).**

Contemporary thinking has it that an appropriate environment is the single most important factor in a successful preservation program. Excessive or erratic heat and humidity will have their way with library collections, even as materials sit quietly on the shelves. Thus, the building manager's job of establishing standards for the library's environment is an important one. He or she will also monitor heating, ventilation, cooling, and filtration systems, using the proper instruments. The following five steps are crucial aspects of the building manager's job.

1. *Understand the library's environmental systems.* A library's heating and cooling system may be steam or electric, overhead or perimeter, on-site or located remotely in a centrally operated plant. In cases where the original building has been extended, *multiple* HVAC systems may exist, each controlling different spaces. An area housing rare books or archives may also have separate controls, and getting to know the library's environmental systems is the building manager's first challenge. Here the building's occupants can be of considerable help: they know how the system *behaves*, offering valuable clues to how it *works*.

2. *Set standards for the library environment.* The two biggest factors in decision making for temperature and humidity are (1) the preservation of materials and (2) the comfort of library patrons. The incredible inroads into library collections made by electronic information justify the inclusion of a third factor: (3) the presence of large numbers of computer workstations. Fortunately, compromise is possible, and there is no shortage of books and articles to guide the building manager on the topic of temperature and relative humidity (RH). Typical recommendations are

sixty-five degrees, plus or minus five degrees, and 25 percent, plus or minus 5 percent (a shift from the 45 percent to 50 percent recommended for many years). The building manager must understand, however, that these standards will be beyond the reach of many libraries: older systems may be mechanically incapable of meeting them, and the cost of building them into new construction may prove much higher than one might think.[4] Furthermore, the finer the degree of control, the more costly it will be to operate the system once it is installed. Again, *compromise* and the ability to accept and work within limits the library cannot control are critical, as is a willingness to balance the costs of building and operating mechanical systems against strict conservation criteria. Whatever the library's environmental systems, the building manager will aim to keep them running constantly, even when the library is closed, because a *consistent* or *stable* climate is generally considered to be more important than a perfect one.

3. *Monitor the library environment.* There is a connection between temperature and humidity: when one shifts, the other will as well. Environmental recording devices will tell the building manager whether temperature and RH are properly regulated. He or she can then make or request adjustments accordingly. Hard data, such as that collected by properly calibrated equipment, can be worth their weight in precious metals if problems arise: facilities management staff are hard-pressed to quarrel with information recorded by psychrometers, hygrometers, data loggers, and similar machines. Even simple tools like thermometers and humidity indicator strips can provide useful data. The building manager will also monitor any filtration system (designed to remove dust, pollution, and dirt from the library's air) installed in the building.

4. *Ensure that environmental systems are well maintained.* Library HVAC systems do not maintain themselves, any more than do those in private homes. The building manager ensures that heating, cooling, and filtration systems are regularly inspected and that air-conditioning and other filters are replaced according to schedule.

5. *Maintain the library building so that environmental systems work effectively.* Even the finest environmental systems can be undermined by a building that works against them. The building manager ensures that doors and windows leading to the outside are kept closed and that windows and doors have efficient seals. Often library staff do not understand the importance of such measures or precisely how the building's environmental systems work: someone who feels too warm is apt to seek relief by propping open a door or window. Here, the building manager has an important staff education task.

• **Supervise housekeeping activities.**

The building manager must monitor the work of the library custodial staff by

- *devising assignments* (vacuuming or mopping floors);
- *scheduling the intervals at which various tasks are performed* (how often will the wastebaskets be emptied and the trash removed?); and by
- *ensuring that staff are well trained,* so that each assignment is carried out in a preservation-friendly manner (there is more than one way to wash a floor—splashing should be discouraged—and the newly hired custodian may need both instruction and explanation in the right approach).

• **Manage library lighting systems.**

There is ample documentation that natural and artificial light containing high ultraviolet (UV) levels are harmful to library materials. Levels can be measured using a simple UV monitor. The building manager should protect the collections from direct sunlight using shades, blinds, or curtains. He or she must take steps to use incandescent lighting (with its lesser UV levels) in stack areas and to keep the lighting low there. In some settings, motion detectors that turn off lights when no reader is present may make sense. Fluorescent lighting can be filtered (and the filters changed at appropriate intervals), as can windows through which strong sunlight streams.

• **Ensure that library shelving meets basic preservation standards and guidelines.**

Even the shelving on which the collection sits is an important aspect of its preservation. Stack surfaces should be smooth, so that books slide over them easily and without injury. Shelves should be adjustable, allowing for a wide range of volume heights. Consider the following four shelving tips.

1. *Wood shelving.* Shelving made of wood may invite insects or release substances that damage the items it should instead protect. It can also splinter and abrade bindings. Depending on the wood's makeup, shelves may sag and their contents with them. Whenever possible, a library should avoid wood shelving. If it must be used, the shelves should be coated with a *noninteractive* substance, that is, the substance should emit nothing capable of penetrating and injuring bookbindings and papers.

2. *Metal shelving.* Even metal shelving can be problematic when it does not meet guidelines for stress, seismic responsiveness, and finishes. Stack finishes should be noninteractive. On metal shelving, some baked enamel finishes and most powder coatings meet this criterion. Some experts recommend uncoated anodized aluminum shelving even more highly.[5]

3. *Compact or high-density shelving.* If compact shelving is closed too rapidly, if ranges are too tall or lurch along their tracks, there is a real danger that volumes or other items may be thrown to the floor (perhaps striking a reader or a staff member on the way down). Minimally, the fragile contents of archival boxes may be shaken and injured. The library should test any manufacturer's shelving, fully loaded with the type of material it plans to house, before making a selection.

4. *Other types of housing for collections.* Staff in units that provide access to special formats often select the housing for these materials: microforms, photographs, maps, compact discs, videotapes, and so forth. However, all types of cabinets, cases, and shelves in the library should meet the general guidelines outlined above.

• Develop and implement a no-food-and-drink policy.

Although the building manager will not want to develop a no-food-and-drink policy independent of consultation with the library administration and other staff, as the person responsible for the building's cleanliness and maintenance, he or she should certainly have a strong voice and can take the lead. Strict preservationists will be unmoved by any suggestion that compromise with regard to food and drink is possible. But the building manager must ask whether it is realistic or desirable to adopt a policy that cannot be enforced or whose enforcement costs more than the potential damage caused by the absence of a policy. A library might stand firm against food but compromise on drinks (especially if these are contained in spill-proof mugs). But the following conditions may make it impossible to enforce such a policy:

- The library is spread out on multiple floors and many areas have no immediate staff presence to enforce a "no-food-and-drink" policy.
- Library staff are reluctant to tell offenders to remove from the building whatever they are eating or drinking.
- No assistance in enforcing a "no-food-and-drink" policy is available from security officers.
- The library cannot hire staff for the purpose of enforcement. The building manager may instead recommend that the library would be better served by frequent trash pickups and removals.

• Implement and monitor a pest control program.

Many of the components of which books and other library materials are made (paper, glue) look like lunch to microorganisms, insects, and rodents. The building manager will probably opt for what the literature of preservation calls an Integrated Pest Management (IPM) program (good housekeeping combined with traps and other nontoxic deterrents). The library's parent organization likely employs an exterminator whose services the library can use, and it will be important to ensure that the chemicals employed (presumably safe for use around humans) are never applied directly to library materials. In some circumstances, it may be necessary to bring in an exterminator who specializes in library and museum work.[6]

Monitoring the building for pests is an important aspect of any IPM program, and here the building manager will require the assistance of other staff, particularly stack maintenance employees, who will be the first to notice mold or insect damage and signs of mice. Likewise, circulation staff must be vigilant in examining returned library materials. Acquisitions and collection development staff also have an important role to play in any IPM program: it is their job to ensure that gift collections (which may contain insects and their egg cases or mold that can spread to adjacent materials) are thoroughly screened and treated before they are integrated with the existing collections.

- **Maintain a stock of emergency supplies.**

It was mentioned earlier in this chapter that facilities management staff are often the first to discover an emergency—flood or fire—in the library. Just as babies seem to be born inconveniently, in the middle of the night, library emergencies tend to occur when the library staff have gone home. One or more prominently located and labeled emergency supply cabinets—containing such things as plastic drop cloths to protect materials from surging water—will repay the building manager's trouble many times over. She or he should ensure that library staff, facilities management staff, and local police and fire department personnel know where the cabinet is located and how to use the supplies it contains. Posted conspicuously inside the cabinet's doors will be a list of library staff names to contact when a disaster occurs after hours.

BASIC SUPPLIES

To Get Started and to Keep on Hand

Plastic sheeting to protect collections and equipment from water

Tape and waterproof markers

Rubber boots and gloves for protection from water

Flashlights with batteries

Camera with film

Office supplies: paper, pencils, pens

Phone lists of staff and local assistance[7]

• **Monitor the library's protective systems.**

The library will have any number of protective systems—sprinklers, fire extinguishers or other fire-suppression devices, water detectors. The building manager will monitor these systems, ensuring that they remain in good working order and that, when appropriate, staff know how to operate them.

• **Oversee security measures and operations.**

The library's security systems protect readers, staff, and materials. From a collections standpoint, security is important because replacing library materials is expensive: the items themselves cost money (assuming they are still available for purchase), as does the staff time to order, catalog, and process them. Furthermore, readers are frustrated when they find items missing but not charged out: unfortunately, some will take out these frustrations in a damaging and inappropriate manner on other parts of the collection. The building manager can take these four steps:

1. *Coordinate and cooperate with the parent organization's security force*, where one exists. Such cooperation is likely to include

   • coordinating the library's key system,
   • monitoring a central security console and the associated services (alarm response policies and actions), and
   • staffing the library with security officers.

2. *Ensure that mechanical security systems are adequate to the library's needs and that they are effectively maintained.* Mechanical systems may include the following:

   • Book detection gates
   • Doors, locks, and window grills
   • Entrance and exit alarms on doors leading to the outside
   • Cameras and motion detectors that deliver information about activity within the library to a central security console

3. *Ensure that staff with security responsibilities perform their duties effectively.* Depending on the library's size and needs, security staff can range from a student positioned at the door to a school library, checking peers' bags and backpacks, to members of a campus or corporation's uniformed security force. Security staff may

   • deny admission to unauthorized users,
   • turn aside someone attempting to bring a picnic into the library,
   • check books and bags when readers exiting the library set off security alarms,
   • respond when alarms, cameras, motion detectors, or other emergency devices indicate unwanted activity in the library, and

- secure doors and windows and remove unauthorized persons from the building at closing time.

4. *Work with special collections staff to develop and implement exceptional security measures for these materials.* These are discussed at some length in chapter 10, "Special Collections and Archival Materials." The Association of College and Research Libraries' "Guidelines for the Security of Rare Books, Manuscripts, and Other Special Collections" will be helpful here.[8]

- **Develop and provide staff training related to the library building.**

The building manager cannot be all places at all times: he or she must rely on the eyes and ears of other library staff to recognize and raise the alarm about environmental problems (mold, moisture, and so forth). The training the building manager develops should address the security of both people *and* collections and may include videotapes as well as workshops.

- **Work closely with contractors to protect the collections during construction projects.**

Even a *small* construction project has the potential to create a *big* preservation problem: for instance, contractors who are trenching a concrete floor for computer wiring get too warm. To admit cool air, they tear down the construction barrier between the site (where air vents have been sealed) and the rest of the library (where air vents are open). Concrete dust is immediately sucked into the building's ventilation system and distributed throughout the entire library. As a result and at a cost of thousands of dollars, the building's air-handling system must be cleaned, as well as every book, shelf, and surface in the library. To help prevent such needless disasters, the library building manager must take the following four steps:

1. *Ensure that collection protection is part of the contract between the library's parent organization and the builder.* The contractor (or his or her insurer) should be responsible for any damage that occurs, including the preservation consultant's expenses and fees. If collections are to be moved, the specifics of their handling and protection from dirt and debris should be carefully spelled out, including specifications for containers (boxes, book trucks). Different provisions will probably be made for different collections—general circulating materials, archival and other special collections, microforms, and so forth. (For more advice on moving collections, *see* the bullet that follows.)

2. *Write into the builder's contract certain preventative measures designed to protect the building's environment and collections.*

3. *Require construction management and security personnel to be present at all times work is under way.*

4. *Arrange for a foreman or supervisor to inspect the construction area daily.* He or she will confirm that the site (including all ducts, air supplies, and

returns) is completely sealed off from the rest of the building and that no particulate matter can be introduced into the air-handling system.

- **When collections are moved from one location to another, provide for their protection.**

Collections may be shifted for a variety of reasons.

- The library decides to relocate humanities materials to a different floor in the building.
- A new science library has been completed, and the associated collections are to be moved to that location.
- The library building is being renovated—furniture, equipment, collections, and staff are to be relocated to temporary quarters for the duration of the project.

Although many of the concerns associated with moving collections relate to planning and sequencing, important preservation issues also present themselves.

1. *Select a qualified mover.* It may be possible to accomplish a small move using staff labor. Here, stack maintenance employees can provide the necessary training in handling the materials. But when outside assistance is required, staff should assure themselves that each company given serious consideration is an experienced mover of libraries and library collections (as opposed to, say, homes or offices and their contents). The mover's staff should be well trained in the handling and transport of library materials, the company chosen able to provide excellent references from other library clients.

2. *Ensure that the containers used for the move safeguard the materials within.* Depending on the size and complexity of the move, many different material types may be involved—bound volumes, microforms, sound recordings, and so forth. The enclosures, book trucks, or other devices used to move each format should adequately protect it from weather, abrasion, and all other types of damage.

3. *See to it that collections move* directly *from the old location to the new one.* Materials should not be allowed to sit for any period of time in intermediate areas—the mover's truck, for example—where they may be exposed to damaging temperature and humidity shifts or extremes, vermin, or theft. (Books subjected to wet conditions or high humidity may bring mold or mold spores with them to their new location. There, the spores can blossom and infect other areas of the collection.)

4. *Provide for the security of collections during the move.* The mover should be bonded and security provided at both ends of the move—in the space *from* which the materials are moved and the one *to* which they are moved.

5. *Provide protection for collections that must be moved into a space that is still under construction.* Ideally, construction will be completed before collections are moved into new spaces. But in real life, building projects often experience delays, and libraries may be required to meet rigid service-related deadlines (school starts September 1). This may mean moving collections into what is still a construction zone, with all the associated dust and dirt. One approach to providing protection under these circumstances is to require the mover to shrink-wrap ranges of materials until construction ends.

6. *Make special provisions for valuable or fragile materials.*[9] Depending on the extent of a library's special collections (rare books and archives, for example), staff may wish to take the following steps:

   • Pack and move the collections themselves. Moving is expensive, both in terms of staff time and packing materials. Staff will want to be aware of, and plan carefully for, the costs of the project.

   • Supervise the packing and moving of such materials. This can extend to traveling with the materials to their new location and ensuring that they are properly arranged there.

   • Ensure that the contents of boxes or cartons are protected from theft.

   • Develop a separate and much more restrictive request for proposal (RFP) for moving these materials. The library might, for example, require the use of climate-controlled vehicles. The company that wins this contract may be different from the one chosen to move the general collections.

7. *Monitor the move, ensuring compliance with all provisions of the mover's contract.* The building manager should assume an active oversight role in the move, maintaining visibility and close contact with the moving company's supervisors.

8. *Use the move as an opportunity to clean and inspect the collection.* Depending on how complex a move is, each affected volume may be handled anywhere from two times to many times. When the staff accomplishing the move can also be trained to (1) dust or vacuum the collections before reshelving materials in their new location and (2) recognize and set aside damaged items for review by library staff, additional benefits will accrue to the library. For more on collection cleaning, *see* chapter 4, "Circulation and Stack Maintenance."

Notes   1. Barbra Buckner Higginbotham, *Our Past Preserved: A History of American Library Preservation, 1876–1910* (Boston: G. K. Hall, 1990), 27.

2. Nancy Gwinn, "Politics and Practical Realities: Environmental Issues for the Library Administrator," in *Advances in Preservation and Access*, vol. 1, ed. Barbra Buckner Higginbotham and Mary E. Jackson (Westport, Conn.: Meckler, 1992), 140–42.

3. The site survey is one of several preservation-related assessments to be mentioned in this book. Readers should not confuse building, environmental, and custodial surveys with collection condition or preservation needs surveys, which are discussed in the chapter on collection development. There are some advantages to securing the services of a consultant to conduct building surveys; these are discussed in Sherelyn Ogden's *The Needs Assessment Survey* [Online], (Andover, Mass.: Northeast Document Conservation Center, 1999 [cited 5 January 2001]); available at <http://www.nedcc.org/plam3/tleaf13.htm>.

4. A recent architects' survey of new libraries showed that HVAC systems that provided for five- to six-degree year-round temperature variations were common, and several new buildings allowed for variations of up to eight to ten degrees. In terms of relative humidity, systems that permitted variations of 25 percent to 30 percent were fairly typical, although some allowed for a range of as much as 35 percent.

5. Sherelyn Ogden, *Storage Furniture: A Brief Review of Current Options* [Online], (Andover, Mass.: Northeast Document Conservation Center, 2000 [cited 5 January 2001]); available at <http://www.nedcc.org/plam3/tleaf42.htm>.

6. A library administrator once asked security staff to visit the dormitory room of a student who had hundreds of titles charged to her but who was unresponsive to overdue notices and telephone calls. There the officer discovered something that resembled an enormous entomology experiment: insects of every type and size swarmed over, through, and among piles of the library's volumes. The university exterminator was summoned, but his preparations only served to *stimulate* the creatures: rather than expiring, they simply ran about more speedily and erratically. At that point, a specialist in library and museum infestations was called in, and the situation was quickly brought under control with no additional harm to the materials in question. Many books were too badly damaged to be saved. Others were cleaned, frozen (to destroy lingering egg casings), rebound, and repatriated.

7. Miriam Kahn, *Disaster Response and Planning for Libraries* (Chicago: American Library Association, 1998), 114.

8. Association of College and Research Libraries, "Guidelines for the Security of Rare Books, Manuscripts, and Other Special Collections" [Online], (Chicago: Association of College and Research Libraries, 1999 [cited 5 January 2001]); available at <http://www.ala.org/acrl/guides/raresecu.html>.

9. Kris A. White's article "Round 'Em Up, Move 'Em Out: How to Move and Preserve Archive Materials," *Conservation Administration News* 57 (April 1994): 16–17, provides helpful information on meeting the preservation needs of archival materials during a move.

3

Collection Development
and Acquisitions

I n many libraries, collection development and acquisitions are closely
linked: librarian subject specialists choose new materials for the collection and make repair, bind, and reselection decisions when damaged
materials present themselves. This work triggers the activities of the acquisitions staff, who choose vendors, place orders, and receive new materials
when they arrive.

Collection Development

Collection development work consists of more than selecting new items for
the library's shelves. In fact, selection is only one aspect of collection development (or what we might think of as collection *shaping*), which also
includes pruning materials that are no longer relevant and the ongoing
assessment of the *condition* of the collections. The librarian placed in charge
of one or more areas of the book stock (and other media that treat the same
discipline) has the broad and critical assignment of

1. *identifying and adding suitable titles,*

2. *deselecting those that are no longer germane, and*

3. *ensuring that materials are in a good and usable state.*

Put another way, selection is only the *first* step in collection development: one
cannot assume that, once selected, a title will always be part of the library collection (absent a decision to withdraw it). Indeed, most materials will not
endure, unless they are properly monitored and provided the necessary care.

A holistic view of collection development vests in the selector responsibility for both the *content* and *condition* of the subject areas assigned to him or her.

• Prepare a collection development policy.

The first chapter in this book addressed the library's need for both a mission statement and a collection development policy, before staff begin planning a preservation program. Librarians with selection responsibilities will provide leadership in creating and maintaining this policy document, attuning it to shifts and changes in the library's mission. The collection development policy follows and reflects the organization's mission statement: here, the library describes the subject areas (biology, literary criticism) and formats (sound recordings, microforms) it acquires as well as collections of particular cultural, research, or monetary value. The chapter "Microforms, Sound Recordings, Video Formats, and New Media" outlines questions a library might ask as it considers the role of various formats in its collections. The "Resource Guide and Bibliography" includes guidance for building a collection development policy.

• Develop a collection retention plan.

On the heels of the collection development policy comes the collection retention plan. In advance of an emergency, librarians should develop recovery, retention, and discard priorities for each major collection—and floor plans indicating where these collections are located. This makes good sense: in the midst of an emergency, when saving the library is paramount in everyone's mind, it is all but impossible to rescue collections and set priorities for their recovery at the same time.

Collections' *worth* (whether expressed in terms of monetary value or cultural significance) and *medium* (film, photographs) will be key factors in assigning priorities. As a part of any preservation needs assessment or collection condition survey, subject specialists can assist the process of assessing worth by assigning value to individual items.

• Select titles that are durable and made from quality materials.

Selection triggers a protracted and costly chain of related events for the library—ordering, receiving, cataloging, processing, housing, circulation, and, of course, preservation. Often an item is available for purchase in multiple versions. When the selector chooses one soundly made from quality materials, she or he can help postpone the day when the library must reinvest in the title because it is damaged or worn. The following four are among the decisions librarians will make:

1. *Which of several editions that will meet the library's needs is most durable.* Where choices exist, the selector can elect an edition printed on permanent and durable paper.

2. *Whether to buy in hardcover or paperback.* The collection development policy may address this issue. Alternatively, the librarian will make a decision based on each title's anticipated use and its continuing value to the collection. He or she will also consider whether the cost of sending a book to the bindery, including staff time, cancels out savings achieved by buying the title in softcover.

3. *Whether to send paperbacks routinely for binding, before they are cataloged and processed.* Here again, usage and worth will be key factors. This issue, like the one above, may be addressed by the library's collection development policy.

4. *When to purchase or license digital versus print information.* Typically libraries are *licensing* electronic text from publishers: they are not *purchasing* it, as they do print and other formats. They do not own it, and this makes it impractical for them to assume responsibility for archiving it. At the same time, the publishers of online information resources are unlikely archivists for their wares. Recent information has economic value, but that of older material is less certain: the creators of digital information may well have a smaller incentive to preserve these resources. Furthermore, questions of publisher continuity (a business folds; one press acquires another) and skills (archiving digital materials is a costly and complex operation) also intervene. (The motion picture and music businesses are cardinal, cautionary examples of the losses that can occur when we assume that those who produce resources will also preserve them.)[1] Until a good model is found for preserving digital information, perhaps in the form of a series of digital archives that would include both libraries and publishers, libraries are best served to opt for electronic formats fully aware of all the caveats.[2]

- **Weigh the preservation implications of gifts.**

A librarian considering a gift collection weighs many factors among the costs associated with accepting the materials. Such costs include those of searching the gifts in the library catalog, as well as cataloging, processing, and housing them.[3] But gifts can also carry substantial and immediate preservation costs, and subject specialists will want to include these four considerations in their thinking:

1. *Can the library provide a climate and surroundings suitable for the gift?* If the library's environment is a poor one—stacks are not cooled in summer; there is no humidity control—in good conscience a librarian may not be able to accept a valuable or fragile gift.

2. *Are the titles damaged by mold or insects?* Under most circumstances, such material will be rejected.

3. *Are the costs of preservation likely to exceed the value of the gift?* If a title is in poor condition, this may well be the case.

4. *If a title is printed on brittle paper, is it worth adding to the collection?* Such volumes cannot be rebound, and even a small amount of handling may make them unusable. Preservation options for such materials are not inexpensive.

• **Make well-informed reselection decisions.**

Worn, damaged, fragile, and lost materials—books, maps, sound recordings, reels of microfilm—regularly present themselves for reselection. Using his or her knowledge of the collection and the use that individual items will receive, the librarian must decide whether titles are to be withdrawn, replaced, repaired, or perhaps reformatted as a preservation microfilm or photocopy. The librarian charged with budgeting for collection development must allocate funds for replacements. (Some formats, like microfilm, will be replaced almost routinely, rather than repaired.) Each choice a librarian makes has its own resource implications, and effective decision making requires training and an understanding of all the alternatives. The following six are among the choices; they include some circumstances under which one might elect them.

1. *Withdraw.* The selector judges the fragile, lost, or damaged item no longer important to the collection.

2. *Repair or rebind.* Pages may be loose or the spine torn, but strong paper and good margins make the item a candidate for mending or a new binding. (*See also* chapter 5, "Binding, Repair, and Reformatting.")

3. *Replace.* A book is badly mutilated and missing pages, but either a quality reprint or microform is available.

4. *Reformat.* Paper is too brittle for rebinding, yet the book has considerable value to the collection. No replacement is available for purchase in either print or any alternative format (microfilm, for example). (For more on reformatting, *see* "Make decisions about reformatting library materials," below, and chapter 5, "Binding, Repair, and Reformatting.")

5. *Provide a protective enclosure.* The paper is too brittle for rebinding, yet the book has considerable value to the collection. Reformatting is not a suitable option, because the title has artifactual value and should be preserved in its original form. At the moment, no funds are available for conservation treatment.

6. *Provide conservation treatment.* The item has artifactual value and should be preserved in its original form. The library has sufficient funds for conservation treatment, which might include cleaning and deacidification.

• **Design and conduct collection condition and needs assessment surveys.**

In an earlier chapter, building surveys (site, environmental, and housekeeping) were discussed. Collection condition and needs assessment surveys are another critical aspect of the library's preservation program.[4] Simply put, these surveys tell the library which parts of its collection (based on a number of factors) should receive priority for preservation. Most foundations and grant-giving organizations will not provide funds for treating collections or correcting preservation deficiencies until a library has conducted a general collection condition or needs assessment survey. (Often funding agencies provide two tiers of grants: the first supporting a survey, the second supporting corrective measures.)

Because external preservation support all but presupposes a general collection condition or needs assessment survey, such a tool is vital to a successful preservation program. The completed survey will show both the *type* and *degree* of damage sustained by different areas of the collection and where brittle paper is most prevalent. With needs assessment surveys, the library augments these data with usage (circulation) statistics, information about collecting strengths, knowledge of research or other valuable collections, and other data, establishing priorities that shape preservation activities and grant writing.[5]

Depending on the size and complexity of the library's collections, survey data may be collected for every item the library owns or for a sample of materials. (When a section of the collection is to be comprehensively surveyed, collection development staff might request that the stack maintenance unit first clean and shelf read the materials and that cataloging staff inventory them.) Often selective surveying is the method of choice: staff handle a representative sample of the collection, rather than taking a census of every item, then use formulas to suggest the percentage of materials in various disciplines that exhibit particular problems. Views about sample size and selection method vary; however, preservation literature on this topic abounds, and this book's "Resource Guide and Bibliography" provides guidance.

Collections with special characteristics (rare books, pamphlets) or distinctive formats (microfilm, maps, posters) will probably be separately surveyed. Data collection forms may be completed and analyzed using a software program.[6] Depending on the size of the collections, staff may use portable notebook computers as part of the data gathering process, taking them into the stacks directly to the site of the materials to be surveyed. The following seven sets of questions may help the library choose which information to collect.

1. *Is the item still part of the library's collection or has it been lost?*

2. *What is the physical condition of the item?*

   - Is it soiled?
   - Has it sustained water, insect, or other damage?
   - Is it missing pages or other parts?
   - Is its paper brittle?

3. *Does the item have significant artifactual value?*

- Is the title unique or scarce?
- Is it likely that other libraries in the city, state, region, nation, or world own this same title?

4. *Should the item be transferred to another collection within the library?*

- Is a book that is part of a circulating collection special in some way— is it a first edition or fine binding?
- Does it contain valuable illustrations?
- Does its provenance make it exceptional?

5. *How frequently or recently has the item been used?*

6. *What is the condition of the environment where the item is housed?*

- Is the area air-conditioned?
- Is it protected against fire?

7. *Is the item properly housed?*

- Is it shelved on its fore edge (that is, spine facing upward)?
- Does it sit inside a rusty cabinet?

A needs assessment survey will give the library as well as prospective funding agencies a picture of the collection's strengths, formats, condition, usage, and storage conditions, one that suggests clear priorities for preservation. It may also generate reselection decisions for librarians with collection development responsibilities.[7]

• Identify and participate in cooperative preservation programs.

Cooperative collection development programs have a venerable history: typically, libraries agree to assume responsibility for certain disciplines or subdisciplines, freeing their partners from this obligation and enabling them to support other types of collections. Favorable on-site and lending agreements for all participants are commonly part of such arrangements. An extension of these collecting partnerships are cooperative preservation initiatives, where libraries assume responsibility for preserving whatever they have agreed to collect. The consortium may also sponsor access to the services of a conservation, microfilming, or digitization center that offers members favorable rates.

These arrangements can be local, regional, national, or international. An underlying aim may be preserving the literature of entire disciplines, rather than just local collections. Librarians must look carefully at the potential benefits before committing themselves to others for the preservation of parts of their collections: local and consortial preservation needs can sometimes collide, and the library may find itself obliged to spend scarce preservation dollars on materials that are not its top priority.

- **Make decisions about reformatting library materials.**

What happens when a title is too fragile, dirty, or damaged to be repaired or rebound, yet no replacement is available for purchase? Even smaller libraries probably own fragile local records that merit microfilming if they are to continue to be used by researchers. These items are candidates for reformatting (copyright law permitting), and collection development staff have an important role to play.

1. *Determine which format will best meet readers' needs.* The most popular options include preservation-quality microfilm and photocopies. For the present, digital copies are best viewed as a means to increase access to collections, rather than preservation formats.[8]

2. *Decide whether or not to retain the volume after photocopying or filming has taken place.* In some cases, the library will wish to retain the original after reformatting has occurred. A subject specialist should make this decision, considering any artifactual or cultural value the original may have.

3. *Determine whether a preservation microfilm already exists.* Before sending a volume for filming, staff should check the databases of major bibliographic utilities and other sources of information to determine whether another copy of the title has already been reformatted. In such cases, the library need only order a service copy for its collections.

4. *Identify a company whose services and products meet accepted guidelines and standards for permanence, durability, and fidelity.*[9] Visiting the service center is one way of answering questions like these:

   - Will the materials (film or paper) the vendor uses last and hold up well under usage? (This means silver gelatin film for preservation and print microfilm masters, alkaline paper for photocopies.)
   - Equally important, will the copies accurately represent the content of the original?
   - Can the vendor house microform masters in a suitable and secure environment? (Some libraries may not be able to provide such an environment themselves.)
   - Is filming equipment modern and well maintained?
   - Is packaging (boxes, reels, ties) sturdy and inert?

5. *Negotiate a contract with a commercial firm or service center.* Typically, volume leads to more favorable terms. It may be that one of the consortial agreements in which the library participates provides for cost-effective access to a service center that films or creates preservation photocopies. The contract should clearly specify the standard to which the vendor will film.

6. *Work closely with staff in other units to ensure that items are properly prepared for filming, photocopying, or digitization and that quality assurance checks are*

performed when the copies are received. Because readying titles for binding and preparing them for reformatting are similar, this book suggests that the work be assigned to the same staff. They will collate items that are to be reformatted, generate targets, dispatch originals to the service center, and review the returned microfilm or photocopies for quality assurance. Collection development librarians will ensure that this work is properly performed. (*See* chapter 5, "Binding, Repair, and Reformatting.")

7. *Ensure that catalog records are appropriately adjusted.* The catalog should reflect either the presence or absence of the original volume and the addition of the title in its new format (microform, photocopy).

• **Build a preservation reference collection.**

Staff in every library unit will have their own preservation responsibilities and educational needs. In consultation with their peers, collection development librarians should build a preservation library that will give all staff authoritative literature they can consult. This book's "Resource Guide and Bibliography" can be mined for ideas.

Acquisitions

Staff in the library's acquisitions unit also play important preservation roles. Once collection development librarians have made their selection decisions, acquisitions personnel take over.

• **Search for and order replacements.**

Acquisitions staff need a good knowledge of both in-print and out-of-print sources of materials. Sometimes it is they who identify replacement options (a new copy, another edition, a different format), informing the selector of his or her options. They should be properly trained to make judgments about the physical quality of available reprints (alkaline paper, quality binding) and replacement formats (microfilm). Following guidelines established by selectors, they may also ascertain the availability of other copies of a title (in the library, within the institution, in the region)—information that may influence reselection decisions.

• **Examine new receipts and return damaged and defective copies.**

Acquisitions staff will carefully check each new title and return defective or damaged titles to the supplier for credit or replacement

1. *Damaged materials.* Not every new book arrives in perfect condition, often because of improper packing and shipping.

2. *Defective materials.* Staff must also learn to examine new receipts for manufacturing defects and construction that is plainly shoddy.[10] Books whose pages already seem eager to pop from their binding should be returned, rather than processed, and another edition or title substituted. Paperbacks often deserve greater scrutiny than hardcovers.

- **Assess the physical condition of gift materials.**

Although new materials (especially those shipped from damp and humid climates) may arrive with mold or insect damage, it is more likely that gifts will evidence such damage. Acquisitions staff will be trained to recognize these problems and immediately segregate affected materials from other parts of the collection. If the damage is serious, subject specialists may reassess the decision to add the volumes to the collection. If they *are* to be retained, they must be appropriately treated.

- **Carefully unpack and handle new materials.**

Boxes of new books (and gift books, too) may be tightly packed, their contents casually wrapped. Acquisitions staff will unpack boxes carefully, taking care not to cut or damage titles near the top. Similarly, they will gently open new books (which are often tight) a few sections at a time and handle materials carefully while they are being accessioned.

- **Place security devices in library materials.**

It is sometimes easy to forget that protecting the collections from theft is a component of any preservation program. In terms of processing materials, this may mean attaching unobtrusive magnetic strips or other objects to them—devices that interact with the library's security gates, causing them to sound an alarm when a reader exits with materials that have not been charged to her or him. Staff will take care never to use such devices with valuable or fragile materials and to avoid placing them on formats (compact discs, for example) with whose usability they are likely to interfere.[11]

- **Search gift collections, passing on to selection officers unique titles.**

Every library will have its own set of guidelines for searching gift collections. Minimally, acquisitions staff will pass on to subject specialists for their decisions titles that are not present in the collections.

- **Substitute gift copies for worn existing copies.**

When duplicate titles are identified in key collecting areas, acquisitions staff will check those in good condition against titles already on the library's shelves, making substitutions as appropriate. Following guidelines established by subject specialists, acquisitions staff may routinely add copies in areas established as particularly subject to loss or theft (film books, extra illustrated books).

Notes

1. Loes Knutson, "The Challenges of Preservation in a Digital Library Environment," *Current Studies in Librarianship* 22 (spring-fall 1998): 66–67.

2. For information about efforts to establish a network of American digital archives, *see* "Preserving Digital Information: Final Report and Recommendations" from the Commission on Preservation and Access and the Research Libraries Group's Task Force on Archiving of Digital Information at <http://www.rlg.org/ArchTF/>, as well as the Digital Library Federation's Web site <http://www.clir.org/diglib/>.

3. If the collection is a large one that seems likely to contain many duplicates, the cost of searching it in the catalog may outweigh the value of the few new volumes the library is likely to add.

4. Some preservationists differentiate between condition surveys and needs assessments. Condition surveys collect more detailed data about the condition of the items that are selected. Unlike needs assessments, they omit risk factors (the library environment and levels of usage, for example).

5. Alternatively, the library can reverse this process by first determining the areas of the collection it deems most important, then conducting condition surveys to identify any preservation problems.

6. Calipr: Preservation Planning Software <http://sunsite.berkeley.edu/CALIPR/> is a popular product and freely available via the Web. References abound in the preservation literature to two other packages: PreNAP—Research Libraries Group's Preservation Needs Assessment Package—and Harvard Surveyor. According to RLG staff, Calipr has replaced PreNAP. Harvard's product is a strictly internal one, unavailable for general distribution and use.

7. There are some advantages to securing the services of a consultant to conduct collection condition surveys; these are discussed in Sherelyn Ogden's *The Needs Assessment Survey* [Online], (Andover, Mass.: Northeast Document Conservation Center, 1999 [cited 5 January 2001]); available at <http://www.nedcc.org/plam3/tleaf13.htm>.

8. Although digitization is an attractive and promising preservation approach (especially for librarians and scholars weary of hard-to-use microfilm), this book does not treat it as a preservation reformatting technique. Rather, digitization is considered as a tool for improving and increasing access to fragile materials. For more on this topic, *see* chapter 11, "Microforms, Sound Recordings, Video Formats, and New Media."

9. Recommended standards and guidelines include those of the Association for Information and Image Management (*see* the *AIIM Standards Program* [Online], (Silver Spring, Md.: Association for Information and Image Management) <http://www.aiim.org/standards.cfm>, as well as those of the Research Libraries Group and the Library of Congress.

10. In his 1990 article " . . . And What Do Librarians Want?" *Publishers Weekly* (June 8, 1990): S12–S16, Robert Carter notes that the New York Public Library reported returning some two hundred volumes each week because they were defective or poorly made.

11. In some libraries, security strips or patches might be added to library materials by processing staff at the same time book pockets, date-due slips, labels, and other attachments are applied. However, the sooner security devices are inserted in new titles, the less likely they are to disappear.

4

Circulation and Stack Maintenance

Circulation and stack maintenance are coupled operations in many libraries. Often the stack maintenance crew is part of the circulation team and reports to the same supervisor. This makes sense, because if a high level of access to the collections is to be maintained, it is critical that returned materials (which come in at the circulation desk) flow quickly and smoothly back to the library's shelves. In many settings, circulation and stack maintenance are part of a larger unit called access services, which is treated separately in this book. (*See* chapter 7, "Access Services.")

Circulation

The circulation desk and the unit it represents are the most visible in the library. Although not every reader will have a reference question or request an interlibrary loan, on any given trip to the library most will charge out or return materials. Each day, circulation staff have a singular opportunity to handle and assess those parts of the collection that are most apt to be in need of care—items that have circulated to readers. If they make good use of this opportunity, they can have a very positive impact on the library's preservation profile.

• Ensure that privilege records are well maintained.

Although maintaining complete and up-to-date records about readers is a greater issue for special collections and archival units than it is for the general library, there will be occasions when good record keeping assists in the preservation of the collections—a reader fails to return his books and the library staff must contact him in order to recover them; when a music score is discharged, some of its parts are found missing. Although a relatively small percentage of preservation problems stem from deliberate damage, on the occasion when this does occur, good patron records are valuable.

- **Examine materials at checkout and return for preservation needs.**

  1. *Remove all extraneous items.* These might include bookmarks, paper clips, pencils, and Post-it Notes.

  2. *Identify damaged materials and flag them for attention.* Even though staff may be working under pressure (perhaps a long line of readers is waiting to return or check out materials or an impatient reader is in a rush), in many cases they can identify books in need of treatment and either put them aside for review by a selector or flag them in the circulation system to be examined upon their return. Staff should be trained to be especially sensitive to signs of mold or insect damage: if infected materials are reshelved rather than isolated and treated, spores may spread or egg casings hatch, disseminating the problem throughout the stacks. In some libraries, circulation staff are trained to determine which books can be mended or rebound and send them directly to the repair or bindery preparation units.

- **When items are discovered to be lost or missing, bring them to the attention of selectors.**

Circulation staff are frequently made aware of titles that appear to be missing from the collection. When a reader wants a book or other item and cannot find it in its assigned location, she or he often asks whether the title is charged to another person. Additionally, many libraries place signs in the stacks encouraging readers to seek assistance at circulation if a book cannot be found on the shelf. Such signs have a dual purpose: to provide good service to readers by improving access to the collections and to control the collections more effectively. Even if a reader does not wish to request a search for a book that appears to be missing—he or she will take another title instead—the information the reader supplies enables the circulation staff to search for the item and either locate it or declare it missing. In the latter case, the title will be brought to the attention of a selector for a replace or withdraw decision.

- **Place books properly on return shelves.**

Just as stack crews must be trained to shelve books properly, so must the circulation staff who discharge returned materials then place them in a staging area before they are arranged on trucks for shelving. Although materials will sit in the staging area for a brief time, compared to the days, weeks, or months they may rest undisturbed in the stacks, they should still be shelved upright, aided by good book supports.

- **Substitute an abundance of open counter space for book slots and book drops.**

Book drops are damaging to all types of library materials and should be avoided if at all possible. Rather than providing drops or slots of any type—whether freestanding outdoor boxes, slots in the outer wall of the library that empty directly into the building, or drop slots in circulation counters—circulation staff should offer readers ample clear and uncluttered counter space where they may stack books they are returning. What are the problems associated with book drops and slots?

1. *Damage to materials.* This damage takes several forms:

    - Books and other materials are often damaged when they enter the book drop. Pages splay open and are torn; spines are twisted. When special formats such as sound and video recordings are added to the mix, a literal stew of broken media can be created.

    - When book drops are located outdoors, the materials in them may be subject to rain and snow, insects and other vermin, as well as dramatic shifts in temperature and humidity.

    - People frequently cram books, cassettes, and other items into a book drop, even after it has reached an overflowing condition: materials are variously damaged, exposed to elements, or free for the taking.

2. *Malicious mischief.* Book drops often encourage pranks or worse. They are inviting receptacles for pranksters.

If the book drop is a fact of library life and cannot be eliminated, staff should consider these four options:

1. *Choose a book drop designed to hold damage to a minimum.* Spring-bottom drops are superior to those with fixed floors.

2. *Empty the book drop often.* The schedule should take into account long weekends when the library may be closed for several days and periods of the year when returns are particularly heavy (the end of the semester, for academic and school libraries).

3. *Keep book drops locked when the library is open.* It is not unreasonable to ask readers to return books at the circulation desk when the library is open.

4. *Eliminate or permanently lock book drops in the library's walls.* These are dangerous devices, in terms of fires and other acts of vandalism. They are also convenient conduits for insects and vermin.

- **Distribute waterproof book bags and other preservation aids to readers.**

Giving readers an acid-free bookmark when they check out materials (perhaps with the library's hours and telephone number printed on it or some preservation information) may keep them from turning down page corners to mark their places or inserting a pencil, paper clip, or other injurious object in the book to achieve this same purpose. This small gift (so common with orders from online booksellers) also suggests that the library cares about its collection.

Similarly, offering readers plastic or other waterproof bags on inclement days conveys the library's commitment to the materials it collects. Even if the message is a somewhat subtle one, it may linger after the rain subsides, causing readers to want to take better care of the items they borrow. If the library cannot afford to buy bags and give them away (they can be attractively imprinted with the library's logo and Web address), perhaps it can share the cost with the public, charging twenty-five cents for a plastic bag that cost fifty cents or two dollars for a cloth one that cost four dollars. This may actually help readers to feel part of the campaign to protect collections. Another option is for staff to bring in the plastic bags in which they carried their groceries home and offer these to readers (providing the bags are clean).

Stack Maintenance

Because no other staff handles the collection as much as the stack maintenance crew (and because this is almost all they do), their training is a very important aspect of the library's preservation program. Because shelvers are often minimum- or low-wage employees, college or high school students, even community volunteers, a special effort may be required to help them develop the appreciation of their work and respect for the collections necessary to their success. The stack maintenance supervisor must understand that the library shelving operation is nothing akin to loading the shelves at K-Mart, where efficiency is the primary goal and if a plastic bottle of shampoo is dropped, it probably bounces with little harm done. (Even if it *is* harmed, it costs far less than the average monograph or videotape.) Finally, the condition of the stacks speaks volumes about the caliber of the library's overall management and its commitment to the collections—a well-run library that cares about its materials has clean, orderly shelves. The stack maintenance crew's key preservation-related responsibilities follow.

• Use safe and sturdy book trucks.

A book truck (also called a cart or trolley) is a valuable preservation tool. Trucks should be selected both for strength and maneuverability. Those with fully movable, rotating wheels roll most easily and smoothly. This is an important feature, because when a cart hits a bump or lurches, books can easily tumble to the floor.

• **Pack and roll book carts safely.**

Library materials on their way for reshelving should be packed securely on book trucks so that, as they roll over elevator entrances, lips joining carpeted and tiled areas, and other obstacles, books do not fall to the floor (or, worse still, down the elevator shaft).

• **Shelve books properly.**

1. *Books should not extend beyond the edge of a shelf.* When they do, they are vulnerable to bumps and abrasion.

2. *Shelve folios and other oversize books separately from the rest of the collection.* Large books should be shelved flat, no more than three or four volumes to a stack, in a separate section of shelving. This prevents them from warping.

3. *Turn leaning volumes upright.* This prevents their shape from becoming distorted.

4. *Correct any fore-edge shelving.* Shelving books on the fore edge (that is, spine facing upward) allows the force of gravity to begin pulling the text block away from the binding. If the stacks are so cramped that some part of the collection cannot be shelved upright, staff should place books spine *down*, rather than spine *up*, even though this means neither they nor the library's clientele can read a book's author, title, or call number.

5. *Use book supports freely and correctly.* Book supports should have smooth, nonreactive finishes. Supports that rest on top of shelves are preferable to the wire ones that clip into the shelf above: it is easy to knife books on such devices.

6. *Do not pack the shelves too tightly.* To do so increases the chance that readers will damage books when they attempt to pull them from the shelves (likely by their headcaps or spine tops).

7. *Identify overcrowded stack areas and report them.* In this way, stack shifts can be designed and scheduled.

8. *Carry out necessary stack shifts.* When parts of the collection outgrow their allotted shelf space and begin to become crowded, the stack maintenance crew shift other materials to accommodate them. Sometimes this can be achieved by moving a few shelves or ranges of materials—making what might be termed a "band-aid shift." But when the library finds itself making a number of such shifts, this is probably a sign that it is time to assess the allocation of growth space *throughout* the stacks and plan a major redistribution of the collections, perhaps adding new shelving at the same time.

- **Identify volumes needing repair, cleaning, or other treatments.**

Through good stack maintenance routines, staff can recognize books that require mending and other treatments, as well as evidence of insect or mold infections, and alert their supervisor so that action can be taken. This task extends to identifying past "preservation treatments" that today are destroying books and other materials—mends with cellophane tape, photographs mounted on acid boards with deleterious adhesives, leather bindings that have been shellacked. After an outbreak of high humidity, shelvers may make regular "mold patrols" in the stacks, looking for outbreaks so that they can be quickly brought under control.

- **Keep an eye out for the general cleanliness of the stacks.**

Are there dust balls or candy wrappers lying around? Are the floors particularly grimy? Staff should report those areas that require special custodial attention.

- **Pick up and reshelve library materials on a regular basis.**

Frequent sweeps keep the library from looking messy, inspiring readers to give the same care to library materials that staff are providing.

- **Keep the collection clean.**

Here, it is important to differentiate the work of the building's custodial staff and its stack maintenance workers. Stack maintenance crews will vacuum and dust the collection (a finer task than cleaning the building), using proper techniques and implements: the soft brush of a vacuum with a HEPA (High Efficiency Particulate) filter gives maximum dust control. "Magnetic" dust cloths attract dust rather than merely recirculating it.[1]

- **Ensure that the stacks have plenty of consultation shelves and step stools.**

These devices are excellent preservation tools. Readers will not walk far to find a flat, smooth space for consulting materials they have pulled from the shelves: if none is nearby, they will prop volumes precariously atop full shelves of books, potentially damaging them. Where step stools are absent, the temptation exists to use a low shelf like the rung of a ladder, to reach materials shelved higher up. This, too, can damage the collections—and injure readers as well.

Note   1. Joyce Frank Watson's "Cleaning Collections," in Moving Library Collections: A Management Handbook, ed. Elizabeth Chamberlain Habich (Westport, Conn.: Greenwood, 1998), 265–72, gives sound advice about collection cleaning.

5

Binding, Repair,
and Reformatting

It is very likely that even the library with no articulated preservation program employs a commercial binder. Over time, many material types will present themselves for the sorts of treatments binderies provide, including volumes damaged or simply worn with time, new softcover monographs, loose journal issues, brittle books, pamphlets, and rare or special materials. Not only has binding technology changed and improved, but so have the methods for controlling shipments that are offered by many vendors: libraries are able to use software to create job lists; specify materials, colors, and fonts; and furnish label content and layout information. Staff will be able to make the most effective binding, repair, and reformatting decisions when they understand the advantages and liabilities of each choice, as well as its cost.

It may be that the employees in a library's bindery preparation and repair units are supporting staff. In that case, these units might report to the head of collection development, who can also assume responsibility for choosing a binder, developing binding policy, building a binding budget—those tasks described below that are clearly the domain of professional staff. (As observed in chapter 3, "Collection Development and Acquisitions," there is a logical relationship between developing collections and ensuring their continued usefulness.)

Binding

After staffing, the largest part of most libraries' preservation budget goes for binding. Because any book's sewing and casing is its primary protection against injury, durable bindings are well worth the dollars expended upon them.

- **Ascertain that the vendor providing binding and other preservation services follows published standards.**

The Library Binding Institute's (LBI) *Standard for Library Binding* is the acknowledged yardstick by which all binding services are measured.[1] The LBI standard suggests that there is no one, single, correct binding approach for every library volume. Rather, libraries should strive for congruence among binding type, binding materials, and the anticipated use of the volume to be bound. This means that the library and the binder share in responsibility for achieving good binding results and that library staff must have a working knowledge of the options the binder can offer.

Because many binders can provide a quality, workmanlike product, the library considering entering into a new binding contract or renewing an existing one may wish to send a sample shipment to several companies, comparing the prices and results achieved. If the library's general binder cannot meet the needs of volumes with special or artifactual value, staff may employ a second and more specialized binder for such materials.

- **Look for a binder who can provide a wide range of services.**

As the number of library dollars available for preservation purposes has grown, many binders have begun providing specialized assistance in this area. Some companies offer mending and conservation services in addition to binding. They may also build enclosures and supply pamphlet binding. Some concerns engage in preservation microfilming and photocopying, deacidification and alkalization, and polyester encapsulation. If the library can find a company that offers a range of quality services, each at a reasonable cost, this is simpler than negotiating multiple contracts with a number of vendors.

- **Negotiate the binding contract.**

The library should examine a number of sample binding contracts before entering into one of its own. Exemplars may be found in various preservation handbooks or obtained from commercial binders or other libraries. In some cases, it may be possible for the library to participate in a joint contract among a number of institutions and a commercial binder; such contracts often offer excellent pricing. The typical binding contract specifies seven elements.

1. *Binding standards.* Here, the contract should follow the LBI standard. The American Library Association's (ALA) *Guide to the Library Binding Institute Standard for Library Binding* will be of help in interpreting and understanding this document.[2]

2. *Binding methods and the type of item to which each will be applied.* These might include oversewing, hand sewing, double-fan adhesive binding, sewing through the fold, or other techniques. The library may specify one binding technique for new softcover titles, another for volumes of periodicals.

3. *Binding materials.* What should be the makeup of materials used for boards, coverings, thread, paper, and adhesives?

4. *The locus of responsibility for determining binding style.* Will the library select the style of binding for each volume it submits (sewn through the fold, double-fan adhesive, hand sewn) or instead allow the binder to place books into broad categories (periodicals, new softcovers, hardcover rebinds)? This decision is a critical one and has clear staffing and cost implications.

   • If the library specifies binding type volume by volume, it is certain (in its judgment) to get the right binding each time. However, the staffing costs for this level of review and assessment can be considerable, depending on the amount of binding.

   • On the other hand, if the binder is given the responsibility of placing each volume into one of a few broadly defined categories, it is probable that general satisfaction, accompanied by a few mistakes, will be achieved. This having been said, it is important to note that most reputable binders have solid decision-making track records. A library can typically rely upon them to call with questions about volumes that seem problematic (very narrow margins) and to identify and return those that are unfit for binding (brittle paper).

5. *Schedules for pickups and deliveries.* Many libraries work on a four-week cycle. The longer the cycle, the greater amount of time volumes will be unavailable for readers' use.

6. *Insurance terms.*
   • For how much will a shipment be insured?
   • How will this determination be made?
   • What procedures will be followed if a shipment is lost or when damage occurs?

7. *The circumstances under which new technologies or materials may be introduced.* Both the library and the binder should consent to any innovation in technique or supplies.

• **Build a sound professional relationship with the binder.**

Two factors make it especially important that the binder bind to the library's satisfaction *the first time:*

1. *Often it is impossible to rectify a binding error.* For example, a book whose margin is severely trimmed cannot have its margin restored, yet the book is no longer of any use.

2. *Commercial library binding has a very small profit margin.* Each time a binder must compensate a library for a damaged book or redo the let-

tering on the spine of a volume of bound journals, the economic consequences are clear.

For these reasons, good channels of communication between binder and library (the primary feature of a sound relationship) are of critical importance. Staff working with the binder should be clear and unambiguous in their instructions and good listeners as well. Once or twice a year, the binder may send a representative to visit the library and meet with staff. He or she will likely solicit feedback and also share information about new developments at the bindery. If distance is not too great a factor, it is also a good idea for library staff to visit the bindery plant.

• Develop the binding policy.

It is important that library staff make binding decisions in the context of a specific policy, rather than as inclination strikes them. The binding policy should mirror the library's mission statement and its preservation policy so that reviewing these documents and placing the binding policy within the same context is a good approach. The purpose of the collection and how it is used will strongly affect the policy, as will the library's size and the nature of its resources.

The binding policy will likely address materials by category. For example, the binding policy as it relates to softcover volumes might state whether the library will

- bind every new paperback,
- bind softcovers only in certain subject areas, or
- bind only after usage suggests that binding would be valuable.

• Develop and monitor the binding budget.

From the binding policy will flow the binding budget. Simply put, what will be the annual cost of following the course of action outlined? It is entirely possible that the library budget may not stretch to cover the amount of work that applying the binding policy will generate. In this case, staff may consider any combination of three actions:

1. *Modify the policy so that it generates a quantity of binding more in keeping with the library's resources.* There may prove to be a gap between an ideal binding policy and a realistic one. (Many libraries couple funds for materials selection and binding, causing staff to think about these two operations as parts of the same whole, collection building.)

2. *Seek an increased annual allocation for binding.* This might be allocated by the director from the library's budget, or perhaps the director can obtain a permanent increase in the library budget to support a binding program.

3. *Obtain a special allocation that will allow the library to catch up on an accumulation of binding.* If binding has been postponed or delayed for some time, or if the library has recently finished a project that generated an unusual number of bindery candidates, perhaps a onetime allocation will allow the library to catch up, making the typical annual figure for binding more manageable.

• **Ensure that staff who make binding decisions are properly trained.**

Staff who manage the library's binding operation must be well trained for their work. Staff making binding decisions should be competent in six areas.

1. *Understand book construction and the use to which each volume will be put.* This will enable staff to talk with the binder in an informed fashion.

2. *Attain familiarity with both the LBI* Standard *and ALA's* Guide to the Library Binding Institute Standard. Here are described such choices as oversewing, sewing through the fold, and double-fan adhesive binding. Staff must have a good comprehension of the strengths, weaknesses, and economics of each method. Money spent on binding techniques that ensure a volume's flexibility represents a good investment—it is almost certain to save dollars later on, in terms of repair and replacement costs.

   • Oversewing is a strong and economical approach, but it hastens the destruction of brittle paper and does not permit a volume to be opened flat (important both for ease of reading and photocopying).

   • Sewing through the fold is expensive but preserves individual signatures and allows a book to open fully and with ease.

   • Double-fan adhesive binding, when used in conjunction with quality polyvinyl acetate (PVA) adhesive, produces a long-lasting and flexible binding at a reasonable cost.

3. *Avail themselves of appropriate training.* Both the LBI and the ALA provide workshops and visual aids to help staff understand binding techniques and materials, and it is likely that the library's binder will also be glad to help out here.

4. *Make decisions in the context of local mission, policies, and anticipated usage.* Unquestionably, different binding decisions will be made in different libraries.

   • Will the library bind periodicals, replace accumulated current issues with microforms, or acquire journals in electronic format?

   • Does the use a softcover reference book will receive justify binding it, or will it hold up until the next edition replaces it?

5. *Recognize when to bind and when to choose an alternative approach.* Depending on the nature of their injuries, books may be sent to the bindery, placed in enclosures, flagged for some other type of treatment, or simply mended. (When a volume's pages are brittle, or exceptionally ragged and dirty, for example, rebinding is likely inappropriate.) It is never improper to consult a subject specialist before making such a decision. ALA's *Guide to the Library Binding Institute Standard for Library Binding* offers a useful decision-making tree that staff may apply.

6. *Specify an appropriate binding style.* Many libraries state in their contracts that such decisions are to be made by the binder. In cases where the library assumes responsibility for specifying binding style, typically the staff will be certain that a particular approach meets the following criteria:

   - It preserves the integrity of the text block (are the margins, for example, so narrow as to suggest a style other than oversewing?).
   - It permits the volume to be rebound again at a later date (trimming the inner margins may preclude this).
   - It enables the book to be opened flat, so that it can be read or photocopied without injury.

- **Prepare materials to be sent to the bindery.**

Books and journals will be sent to the bindery at regularly scheduled intervals (perhaps every four weeks), as specified in the bindery contract. Typically the binder sends a truck to collect the materials, which staff should pack as near to the pickup date as possible. This ensures that readers have maximum access to the library's collection. The assignment of packing materials for the binder includes four steps.

1. *Prepare detailed and accurate bindery slips.* The bindery slip provides a great deal of critical information, including binding style, spine imprint, and so forth. Most binders recommend or even make available PC-based software that enables libraries to generate bindery slips and packing lists via computer, rather than laboriously completing them by hand. Information that will remain the same, shipment after shipment (the color to be used to bind a given journal run, the layout and content of the information to be imprinted on each volume's spine), can be input only once, then reused over and over again. It is not uncommon for a binder to provide his or her library clients with software upgrades and on-site technical support for bindery preparation software, free of charge.

2. *Keep records.* There are several aspects to this task.

   - Staff will record what titles are sent to the bindery, when they were sent, what procedures and materials were specified, and so forth. Software can typically be used for this purpose.

- If software that manages the bindery process does not interface with the library's online catalog, staff also update the catalog record for each title sent to the bindery, indicating its whereabouts.

3. *Collate the shipment.* Staff ensure that monographs are whole—that no pages are missing, that any loose pages have been placed in the volume in the proper order. Similarly, runs of loose journal issues should be complete (or acknowledged to be incomplete, with instructions to bind as is) and placed in proper binding order.

4. *Pack bindery shipments.* Protective and secure packaging ensures that volumes that are already in need of treatment, as well as vulnerable unbound periodical issues, arrive at the bindery in the best condition possible. The binder typically supplies the library with sturdy, reusable boxes, replacing them as use and wear dictate.

- **Receive and inspect returned shipments.**

1. *Unpack the bindery boxes.* This should be done with care, so that the contents are not accidentally damaged with box cutters or other implements.

2. *Inspect returned shipments.* A detailed checklist that assists in this process is contained in *Guide to the Library Binding Institute Standard for Library Binding.* Among the things staff will check are the following:

  - The work meets all standards for materials and style outlined in the binding contract. (Did the library specify sewing through the fold and instead receive adhesive binding? Has a lesser grade of cloth inadvertently been substituted? Have margins been trimmed, despite a "no trim" proviso?)

  - The volumes' appearance is satisfactory. (Have journal volumes been consistently bound in the proper color? Is the labeling on items in a series consistent? Is spine lettering accurate and of the proper size, font, and color?)

  - The volume opens flat. If not, it will likely be damaged as a function of reading it or photocopying it.

  - Every item sent has been returned. Alternatively, the binder has included an explanation for items that are missing.

3. *Update bindery and catalog records.* The bindery records should be annotated, to reflect each item's return. Catalog records must be adjusted, to show that volumes are once again on the shelf and ready for use. (It is likely that staff will also have to add a new bar code to each volume and enter this information in the online catalog.)

4. *Monitor the bindery budget.* Invoices will be returned with each shipment, and these should be used to track the bindery budget.

5. *Return volumes to the library shelves.* It should be possible to save time and bypass the processing unit by having the binder imprint the call number on each volume's spine and allowing staff in the bindery or shelving unit to add such processing products as the library requires—date-due slips, for example.

Repair

Over the course of their lives, many bound volumes are damaged and require repair. Their injuries may include loose covers, signatures with broken sewing, damaged spines, or torn pages. To address them, the text block may be resewn or recased or replacement pages tipped in. Some repair units build enclosures (perhaps for brittle books), such as boxes, portfolios, and wraps. Staff may also encapsulate fragile single sheet items. The byword for effective repairs is *reversibility:* it should be possible to undo any of the work the staff performs, without further damaging the item. (Among other things, this means no cellophane or tapes treated with rubber, whose residues will eventually stain or damage bindings and book papers.) Reversibility can be thought of as preservation's Hippocratic oath: "First, do no harm."

- **Determine whether mending, rebinding, or an alternative approach is appropriate.**

A worn or damaged volume deserves some degree of assessment before it is flagged for repair, rebinding, or replacement. The following four questions should be asked.

1. *Is this volume still relevant in the library's collection?* A subject specialist should look at any book before extensive repair or rebinding is undertaken.

2. *Is the paper good enough to withstand rebinding?* Brittle paper means a book should not be rebound—the pages will only break at the sewing, as they are turned. A brittle book is generally a candidate for replacement, reformatting, or an enclosure.

3. *Does the volume possess artifactual value?* If it does, only a qualified conservator should make decisions about its repair. Many modern binderies have a conservator on staff and offer such services. Until the book can be evaluated, it should be placed in a protective enclosure.

4. *Is the damage such that repair is more economical than rebinding or replacing the volume?* Cost should always be factored into the decision-making process.
   - When the sewing is extensively damaged, rebinding may be less expensive than mending.

- When damage is considerable and of several types yet the book is still valuable to the collection, replacing it or reformatting it may make more sense.

- **Ascertain which is more economical—in-house or commercial repairs.**

Before embarking on establishing and operating an in-house repair center, a library should carefully calculate the associated costs. This means estimating the number of hours to be spent in this work (and the classification and wage levels of the staff who will perform it), as well as necessary expenditures for training, supplies, tools, and space. Staff time will certainly be the largest of these several costs, and many libraries find it more difficult to obtain human resources than any other type. Thus, it may well be cheaper to send materials out for repair (most commercial binderies do such work) than to establish an in-house repair unit, especially if staff time is in short supply or difficult to acquire. (In making this decision, the library will also want to consider the related issue of access to materials: volumes may be out of circulation for a shorter period of time when they are repaired in-house, because bindery shipments typically work on cycles of no fewer than four weeks.)

- **Provide training for those employed in an in-house repair unit.**

There is much more to establishing an in-house mending center than having the necessary funding in hand. Proper technique is a critical element, because creative or uninformed repair techniques often provide results that are injurious rather than beneficial. (The same tape that wraps holiday packages so satisfactorily is quite damaging when applied to the torn leaf of a book.)

For this reason, staff who do repair work should be well trained in every approach they undertake. Although any number of helpful manuals depict techniques for book repair and other activities that may go on in a mending unit, a better approach is to send staff to qualified individuals or concerns for initial training and perhaps periodic retraining as well. For a fee or some other consideration, a commercial bindery, another library with a well-established repair center, or a local conservator will probably be glad to supply hands-on instruction in a range of mending techniques. Alternatively, the library can hire someone already possessing these skills. The repair unit should also establish its own small reference collection containing handbooks that illustrate and describe repair and other techniques the staff will apply.

- **Choose archivally sound supplies and suitable tools.**

It is likely that the paste, scissors, and other supplies and tools the library has on hand are inadequate for the work of a repair unit. Fortunately, many library supply firms offer an archival line, and there are other companies whose sole concern is archival supplies and tools. (Some businesses focus even more sharply on supplies and equipment for specific formats—photographs, for example.) One reliable source for information about where to acquire such products is the Northeast Document Conservation Center's Web site. This book's "Resource Guide and Bibliography" suggests other resources as well.

- **Engage in complete and accurate record keeping.**

Whether the library operates its own repair unit or sends items out for treatment, good record keeping is important. A common repair-rebind slip that can be used by all library units makes good sense. It will tell the mending center (or the staff preparing materials for shipment to the commercial bindery)

- which library unit referred the book;
- where the repaired item should be returned (to cataloging, circulation, or reference);
- the nature of the damage (missing pages, loose text block, torn headcap);
- the name of the referrer; and
- the date of the referral.

- **Delimit the tasks to be performed by an in-house repair unit and those assigned to a commercial bindery.**

Many tasks could be assigned either to a local library repair unit or a commercial bindery, and the library must determine which approach makes the best economic sense. What sort of repairs or other treatments will be performed in-house and which will be referred to the library's binder? The decisions made here will have a real impact on the staffing, training, space, and operating budget allocated to an in-house operation.

1. *Simple book repairs.* These might include

   - surface cleaning of book pages,
   - tipping in replacement pages,
   - repairing spines and hinges, and
   - creating pockets for accompanying items such as maps or diskettes.

2. *More advanced book repairs.* Such work could include

   - mending torn pages,
   - resewing, and
   - recasing.

3. *Building enclosures.* These might include

- boxes,
- portfolios, and
- wraps.

4. *Pamphlet binding.*

- Whether this work is done in-house or sent out, the library will want to specify acid-free binders that employ sewing rather than staples to attach the pamphlet. Staples will eventually rust and cause damage to the pamphlet the enclosure was meant to protect.

- Binding multiple pamphlets together—an approach popular some years ago—is today acknowledged as a mistake: often the paper on which pamphlets are printed is poor, and the acid it contains easily migrates from one item to that bound next to it. Furthermore, when pamphlets of varying sizes are bound together in a single volume, as time passes the binding often begins to sag. This means that it is no longer capable of properly supporting its contents. (Binding pamphlets together also presents serious issues both for access and bibliographic control, but these are outside the scope of this book.)

Reformatting

In chapter 3, "Collection Development and Acquisitions," this book suggests that the tasks of deciding what to reformat, identifying a service center to perform the work, and negotiating a contract be delegated to collection development staff. Because readying titles for binding and preparing them for reformatting are similar, this work can easily be assigned the same staff. Sometimes the same company offers both binding and reformatting services.

- **Maintain complete and accurate records.**

The library will want to track items that have been sent for reformatting—when did they leave the building, and when were they returned? What special instructions were provided to the service center?

- **Collate titles to be sent for reformatting.**

The volume should be complete and its pages in the proper order. This work includes obtaining replacement pages, where this is necessary, by contacting other libraries owning copies of the title. (The service center may be willing to perform this work, for an additional fee.)

- **Generate a target for each item to be filmed or photocopied.**

A *target* is a form created by the library that accompanies the volume to be reformatted to the service center. There, it is filmed so that it appears at the beginning of the reformatted title. It includes the title's bibliographic record. (Sometimes this work is delegated to the vendor.)

• **Pack items and ship them to the service center.**

Items that are so brittle or otherwise damaged that it is necessary to reformat them—preserving their intellectual content but not necessarily their original format—require careful packing, so that they reach their destination in fit condition for filming or copying.

• **Review returned microforms or photocopies for quality assurance.**

Although the filmer or copier is providing quality control services as part of his or her contract and price, some percentage of each returned shipment should be examined to ensure that it meets the standards outlined in the agreement between the library and the service center and that the titles have been filmed completely, in the proper sequence. The Northeast Document Conservation Center provides clear guidelines for such a review in its leaflet "Microfilm and Microfiche."[3] In cases where the library has asked that the volume be returned with the film or photocopy (rather than destroyed), staff will also assess its completeness and condition.

• **Update the library's records and send reformatted items for processing.**

The bindery unit's records, as well as the online catalog, must be updated to reflect the item's return. In cases where the library will create a new bibliographic record for the reformatted item (which is now a reel of microfilm or a photocopy, rather than the original bound volume), the item will be sent to the cataloging and processing unit.

Notes
1. Library Binding Institute, *Library Binding Institute Standard for Library Binding*, 8th ed. (Rochester, N.Y.: Library Binding Institute, 1986).

2. Jan Merrill-Oldham and Paul A. Parisi, *Guide to the Library Binding Institute Standard for Library Binding* (Chicago: American Library Association, 1990).

3. Steve Dalton, *Microfilm and Microfiche* [Online], (Andover, Mass.: Northeast Document Conservation Center, 1999 [cited 5 January 2001]); available at <http://www.nedcc.org/plam3/tleaf51.htm>.

6

❧⟐❧

Cataloging and
Materials Processing

Cataloging and materials preparation are fundamental aspects of any preservation program. Here, the staff's responsibilities sort into two distinct categories: (1) applying the library catalog as a preservation tool and (2) handling and processing materials. The quality of a library's catalog records is of enormous consequence in terms of the institution's ability to recover from an emergency. The accuracy and completeness of the catalog also assists in managing items flagged for preservation treatment and in conducting collection condition and needs assessment surveys. At the same time, cataloging and processing staff are well positioned to identify materials in need of preservation treatment *before* these are sent to the shelves. Their choice of processing materials and the way in which they handle materials in their care are also central to the preservation program.

• **Ensure that the collection is properly cataloged.**

Not only is thorough descriptive cataloging critical for fragile and valuable materials (it reduces the level of random and unnecessary handling they receive), but it serves the preservation interests of general collections as well. Indeed, quality catalog records are part of the firmament of any preservation program: absent a complete understanding of the extent and nature of the collections, how can the library develop preservation priorities? The collections must be comprehensively and accurately described.

• **Keep the library catalog up-to-date.**

If there are large, uncontrolled backlogs of materials awaiting cataloging, or if catalog maintenance is deferred in favor of other activities, both the readers of the present and the future will be poorly served. Indeed, the timely upkeep of the catalog is as important as its accuracy: in the event of a disaster of any significant scale, the catalog is the library's most valuable tool for assessing loss and making replacement decisions.

- **Maintain a duplicate copy of the shelf list.**

An adjunct or subset of the catalog, the library's shelf list contains records of the collection arranged by classification number. The shelf list properly records every volume and copy of a title the library owns. So critical is an accurate and well-maintained shelf list to replacing titles lost in a disaster that the library should keep a duplicate copy in some secure off-site location. When the catalog is computerized and there is no physical shelf list, the library will want to ensure that data of the sort a physical shelf list would contain are backed up regularly.

- **Enhance collection condition and needs assessment surveys by first inventorying materials.**

When a section of the collection is to be comprehensively surveyed for its preservation needs, collection development staff will often request that materials first be inventoried. The reasoning here is simple:

1. *Preservation should be viewed in a comprehensive sense.* If a volume is missing from a section of the collection whose preservation needs are under review, identifying it so that subject specialists can make reselection decisions is one aspect of meeting that section's complete preservation needs.

2. *The entire collection, not just that part sitting on the library's shelves, should be surveyed.* Absent information about materials that are charged out, a snapshot of the collection's condition may be a fuzzy or inaccurate one.

3. *The completeness of the collection is central to preservation decision making.* If some significant portion of the collection is lost or missing, this information may well influence its ranking as a preservation priority.

- **Modify catalog records when materials are removed from the collection for various preservation purposes.**

Preservation activities need not and ought not supersede readers' needs: when titles are removed from their assigned location in the library and queued for some sort of preservation treatment or assessment, cataloging staff will update the catalog's records accordingly. These changes presume an online catalog. It would be impossible to justify making such temporary modifications to manual catalogs. These are four of the circumstances under which staff will modify records in the library's catalog:

1. *A title is to be microfilmed.* As soon as possible after a volume is selected for preservation microfilming, cataloging staff will note the fact in the catalog record (as well as the record representing that title in the

library's bibliographic utility) or create a prospective catalog record for the film that will follow. This is often referred to as *queuing*, a rather misleading term in that it only publicizes the fact that the library intends to have the title reformatted—it does nothing to facilitate that process. Not only will the library want readers to know that a given title is presently unavailable (and slated to reappear in a new format), but it will also wish to alert other institutions (who might consider filming the title themselves) that the task has already been undertaken. In this way, the library community as a whole spends its precious preservation dollars as efficiently as possible.

2. *A title is referred to a subject specialist for assessment.* If it is anticipated that a subject specialist will require any length of time to assess an item's preservation needs or shelf-worthiness, staff should indicate in the catalog record that the material is momentarily unavailable or that the reader should do something to obtain it other than going to the shelf. (Staff may wish to establish a catalog location and associated note that directs readers appropriately.)

3. *A title is sent to the bindery.* Once a volume or group of journal issues is pulled for binding, it will almost certainly be out of commission for several weeks, while staff prepare it for transport, the bindery does its work, and the returned shipment is examined and processed. Catalog records should inform the library's clientele that materials are at the bindery, with some estimate of the time of their return.

4. *A title is sent to the repair unit.* Unless the needed repair is likely to be completed and the item returned to the shelf before the cataloging staff can alter the bibliographic record, or so quickly that the time needed first to adjust, then readjust, the record is clearly unwarranted, the catalog record should be changed to show that a title is temporarily unavailable for use.

- **Revise the library catalog to reflect subject specialists'
  retention decisions.**

Worn and damaged materials regularly require reselection or retention decisions by subject specialists—withdraw a title, replace it with a new edition or another similar title, reformat it, transfer it to special collections, and so forth. It falls to cataloging staff to reflect these decisions in the library's catalog—to withdraw bibliographic records, add new ones, or change locations, depending on the decisions selectors make.

- **Examine materials for evidence of preservation needs
  before cataloging or processing them.**

This activity applies both to new and gift materials.

1. *New materials.* Although acquisitions staff examine new titles for obvious damage and defects, as part of the cataloging process (which includes

collation) library staff are well positioned to identify flawed copies that should be returned to the supplier.

2. *Gift materials.* Here again, acquisitions staff have already checked gifts for visible signs of mold, insect damage, and so forth. Cataloging staff will examine them for more subtle defects, potentially involving the subject specialist in a decision about whether the title should be added to the collection or not.

• **Properly house materials awaiting cataloging.**

Just as collection maintenance staff are charged with the sound housing of cataloged collections, cataloging and processing staff will ensure that materials awaiting cataloging stand upright and are properly supported.

• **Select sound processing materials and supplies.**

Staff should use processing materials and supplies that are consistent with the library's preservation goals.

1. *Get to know the sellers and manufacturers of processing products (inks, pastes and other adhesives, labels, enclosures).* Keep a supply of catalogs from those whose products meet preservation standards.

2. *Order small amounts of each from several likely vendors.* One way of making effective decisions about products is to work with materials from a few manufacturers before deciding on the ones that are most suitable.

3. *Choose inks and adhesives that are nonacidic and nondamaging.* What are the qualities of the paste that is used to attach bookplates or spine labels? Many processing supplies (bar codes, date-due slips, and book pockets, for example) are self-adhesive, and staff should enquire closely of manufacturers about the characteristics of these substances.

4. *Contact manufacturers with questions about their products.* When staff are in doubt about the qualities of processing supplies—whether these are alkaline/neutral/inert, for example—they should contact the manufacturer for information. This can be particularly important for those supplies that may already be on hand. Alternatively, kits that can be used to test the acidity of various processing products can be purchased.

• **Choose suitable containers for all formats.**

The library's most common format, the bound volume, will seldom require a container or enclosure. (Rare or fragile books may, and boxes for these materials are addressed in chapter 10, "Special Collections and Archival Materials.") Any number of books addresses the preservation needs of specific formats—sound recordings or film, for example. (Some of these are included in this book's "Resource Guide and Bibliography.") Among these needs is that for a proper container, and chapter 11, "Microforms, Sound Recordings, Video Formats, and New Media," touches on this topic. Because processing staff may be in a position to select containers, they should keep in mind three general rules that apply to all enclosures.

1. *Choose a sturdy container.* Should a reader or a staff member drop the enclosure, it will be better able to protect the item within and lessen any damage it might sustain.

2. *Select containers made from archival-quality materials.* Whether paper, plastic, or some other substance, all containers should be fashioned from permanent, durable, noninteractive materials. Staff should keep in mind that container selection is not a beauty contest: appearance is of far less concern than strength and stability.

3. *Label containers in a way that indicates how they should be shelved and opened.* Labels should be affixed to boxes and other containers in locations that give the staff who shelve them a clear indication of how they are to be placed on a shelf or in a case—vertically or horizontally, this end up or that end up. Label location can also suggest to readers how and where the enclosure is to be opened.

- **Process materials so that they incur minimal damage.**

By reconsidering their processing routines and devising a few small changes, staff can make a very positive contribution to the library's preservation program.

1. *Avoid straining bindings and damaging pages with foreign objects.* Paper clips, Post-it Notes, and the like have no place in the cataloger's tool kit; they can damage leaves or deteriorate and spoil bindings. This is especially true when books must sit for some time in a backlog before the cataloging and processing operation is complete. Instead, staff can make notations on nonacidic slips of paper and tuck these inside the book, and use white cotton twill tape (instead of rubber bands) when it is necessary to hold the covers of a volume together. Along these same lines, bunches of paper—computer printouts, invoices, and the like—can strain a binding: cataloging staff may wish to review the need for so much paperwork to travel with a book through what can sometimes be an unexpectedly lengthy processing operation.

2. *Apply book jackets in ways that do not damage the book itself.* This means placing the jacket *on* the book but not *attaching* it to the covers so that endpapers are likely to tear or become discolored.

3. *Show restraint and good judgment in the placement of stamps, labels, and attachments.* Processing staff may face the challenge of affixing a dizzying array of labels and other devices to each item that passes through

their hands—property stamps, bar codes, security strips, book pockets, date-due slips, spine labels.

- Reassess the need for each attachment. (In one library, long after the implementation of an integrated library system eliminated the need for book pockets, processing staff were still patiently pasting them onto each volume's endpapers.)
- Keep the number of property stamps to some acceptable minimum. How many times, at how many intervals, in how many places does the library presently require a potentially defacing ownership stamp? Will the level of protection achieved be significantly decreased by reducing the number or location of these stamps? (Of course, the long-term value to the collections of the item being stamped must be factored into such decisions—perhaps one could stamp with impunity *every* page of the bulk of the hundred copies of a new best-selling mystery acquired by a large public library system, in the full knowledge that only one or two of these might be retained in the permanent collection. However, because staff work most efficiently when following guidelines that apply to large categories of materials, some general reduction of the number of property stamps will probably work best.)
- Apply all labels and other attachments so that these interfere as little as possible with text, decorative endpapers, and so forth. By equipping staff with a few commonsense guidelines rather than a series of commandments—giving them the option, for example, of affixing a bookplate somewhere other than the front endpapers, in the event said endpapers are illustrated or folded—the library can improve the integrity of its collections.
- Choose nonacidic ink for stamping property marks, never perforators.

4. *Use pencil rather than pen to record any accessions or other local data in an item.* Inks are often acidic. Over time, they may eat through paper. And, unlike pencil, ink cannot be completely or successfully removed.

5. *Open uncut pages carefully.* This means using the proper tool for slitting pages, rather than just any sharp object (a letter opener, a pair of scissors) typically found on a library work surface.

- **Adopt special procedures for cataloging rare or fragile materials.**

Rare and fragile materials have their own set of processing needs—requirements that are vital for effective preservation. A further complication is that support for preserving such collections may not have been identified at the time staff are ready to catalog them.

1. *Limit the number of staff working on the collection.* Because the materials in question are valuable or fragile, limiting the employees who have access to them to a small, well-trained number is good policy.

2. *Work on only a few items at a time.* Because security is an important aspect of any preservation program, it is a good idea to remove only small groups of special materials from a secure area for cataloging and processing. Certainly no more titles than can be handled in a single day should be taken out in the morning, and these should be returned to a secure area each evening before the staff go home.

3. *Ensure that staff handling special materials are properly trained.* This will include instruction in opening bound volumes, turning their pages, and using book snakes to hold pages open at a given place in the text.

4. *Use alternative, indirect methods for marking and labeling rare and fragile materials.*

   • Staff must never affix any mark of ownership, label, or bar code directly to special materials. If books are to stand or lie on shelves unboxed, then labels, bookplates, and other information can be affixed to acid-free strips placed in the volumes.

   • The labels, bar codes, and bookplates—as well as the paste used to attach them to the strip—should themselves be acid free.

   • Any ink used on the strips should be indelible and nonacidic, so that it neither bleeds onto the volume's pages nor eats into them.

   • Even though the manufacturer warrants processing supplies to be acid free (the paper from which marking strips are made, bookplates, labels, paste, ink), staff should spot-check new supplies for alkalinity: mistakes have been known to happen.

   • When a collection is cataloged before funds are available for a prospective boxing project, bookplates, labels, and so forth will be attached to marking strips. Later, these strips can be laid inside the container. When cataloging and boxing coincide, bookplates and similar markers can also be attached directly to the container itself.

   • If special materials are not ready for use once cataloging is completed, the library may consider shielding their catalog records from the public eye. (Many computerized catalogs offer the ability to create but not publically display a bibliographic record.) This prevents readers from requesting access to fragile materials that are awaiting preservation treatment.

7

Access Services

The units that are part of access services vary from library to library. In larger settings, access services often includes all those public service functions that do not involve a reference component. Sometimes circulation, stack maintenance, and interlibrary loan are part of access services. In this book, access services includes privileges, signage and publications, nonbibliographic reader education, staff education, copy services, and reserves—those functions that permit or promote collection access. Circulation, stack maintenance, and interlending are treated in a separate chapter.

• **Plan and deliver a preservation education program for readers.**[1]

Readers, whether they are young or old, students or scientists, corporate executives or steam fitters, are not born with an appreciation of the needs of books and other library materials.

- A college student leaves his backpack (filled with library books) lying on the quad; later it rains.

- A harried parent does not think about the effect the sun will have on a stack of compact discs left lying in the car's back window.

- Relaxing in the tub at the end of the day, Jane Jones scarcely notices that the bottom edge of the novel she is reading has drifted below the bubble bath's surface.

- "Gee—another great use for Post-it Notes!" thinks Bill Brown, as he shuts the book he's borrowed from the firm's library and rushes off to a meeting.

In some strange way, libraries work *against* the formation of a preservation presence in the reader's mind—the very *existence* of libraries creates a sense of the book's longevity and hardiness. Then, there is the very real fact that we live in a throw-away society: everything from paper cups to disposable diapers (and perhaps even paperback books) teaches people that much of what passes through their hands is not meant to endure. These three factors—(1) people do not understand the preservation needs of library materials, (2) people do not see their personal behavior toward books as much of a threat to the existence of libraries, and (3) many of the tools of modern life are meant to be disposable or easily and cheaply replaced—create a real need for a direct and explicit preservation education program for library users. A good preservation education program can make a significant difference in the number of items presenting themselves for treatment or replacement. To recast this concept in simple economic terms, any library spending significant resources on preservation will want to contain program costs by doing everything possible to reduce the number of items that must be treated. A reader education program includes these four concepts:

1. *Make the program* personally *relevant to readers*. People are most responsive to topics they perceive to be directly applicable to themselves. For this reason, readers may show greater interest in educational programs that nominally address the preservation needs of their own collections—the books, photographs, and sound recordings sitting on their shelves at home—than they do in those aimed directly at caring for library materials. Programs or clinics (a popular term apparently intended to give the instruction a scientific cachet) can teach readers how to handle, shelve, and mend their own materials—with the intention that the skills learned will also be used with the library's collections.

2. *Use educational methods readers are likely to find appealing.*

   - Show one of the many educational videotapes available on the market. (For suggestions, see this book's "Resource Guide and Bibliography.")
   - Ask a local preservation specialist to make a presentation.
   - Invite attendees to bring with them books and other materials from their personal libraries, and advise on their preservation needs.
   - Distribute handouts that demonstrate handling and shelving techniques.
   - Ask a vendor of archival supplies to provide samples of mending materials for distribution to attendees.
   - Plan the program around preserving material of considerable interest to the target audience—for high school or college students, how to handle, load, and house CDs; for the general public, storing and displaying photographs.

3. *Address the needs of all types of library materials.* Plan educational programs for both print and nonprint materials, including books, sound recordings, videotapes and discs, and other film formats. Although it is unlikely that readers have home collections of microfilm, this important library format (and one so easily and innocently damaged) should be maneuvered into other educational programs.

4. *Use a range of tools to deliver the preservation message to readers.* In addition to lectures, hands-on workshops, and videos,

   - add preservation education components (the text of handouts or publications that have been created) to the library's Web site;
   - link to sites that already contain preservation information, like <http://www.nedcc.org>; and
   - if the library Web site includes preservation information, include the library's URL on any publications or bookmarks the library provides.

- **Plan and deliver a preservation education program for staff.**

This responsibility is very much an *optional* one. Not that the existence of a staff education program should be optional—far from it. Rather, the library may find it more efficient to make individual units in the organization the locus for appropriate preservation training. (*See* chapter 1, "The Library Director.") Following the decentralized approach to preservation set forth in this book, the cataloging supervisor would train his staff to process materials in a preservation-friendly fashion, and the stack maintenance manager would ensure that her staff is in command of proper shelving techniques.

But because there will be some elements in a preservation education program that are common to more than one unit (basic book structure and handling, for example), a library may wish to create one or two training modules that can be shared across the organization. Because access services will develop the reader education program (whose elements will have much in common with a program for staff), it makes sense for this unit to build any generally applicable training components.

- **Provide training for the library's preservation partners.**

Chapters 1 and 2, "The Library Director" and "The Library Building Manager," mention a number of partners that should be included in the library's preservation program. Training for these external partners—notably, security, custodial, and facilities management staff—can yield big dividends, particularly if an emergency strikes.

1. *Offer to make presentations at partners' staff meetings.*

2. *Put the emergency preparedness and recovery plan on the library Web site.* Ensure that partners know it is there.

3. *If partners have their own manuals or Web areas, put the library's emergency preparedness and recovery plan there as well.* The fewer clicks needed to access these important data, the better. Minimally, this information will include

- whom to call,
- what to do first,
- library floor plans, and
- where emergency supplies are located.

- **Provide exhibits, posters, table cards, bookmarks, and other tools that assist in the public preservation program.**

Presentations and workshops are good approaches to educating readers about the collection's preservation needs. So are exhibits, posters, table cards, and bookmarks.

1. *Exhibits.* Most libraries have exhibit space that is used to display everything from special collections to materials related to holidays and specially designated months (Women's History Month). There is no reason that preservation causes should not occupy the library's cases for some part of the year. Exhibits might accompany specific preservation programs (how to care for your CDs, books, photographs). A stock-in-trade is the exhibition of damaged materials, alongside illustrations of the perpetrators (insects, rodents, mold, human beings).

2. *Posters.* Many preservation service centers and library consortia, as well as the American Library Association, sell an array of posters promoting various preservation themes—don't eat or drink in the library; protect library materials from the rain; don't use foreign objects as bookmarks. These can be acquired inexpensively and may be persuasive when they are suited to a library's particular clientele. Alternatively, the parent organization's publications or printing unit may be able to generate attractive posters that specifically relate to the institution's mission and purpose.

3. *Table cards.* Sometimes called table tents, these little devices (generally made of heavy paper) are three-sided. One side rests on the table, and the other two face readers seated on either side of it. Table cards are printed with messages for readers—work quietly, do not reshelve books, and so forth. They can also be used to request that the library's clients refrain from eating and drinking. An advantage to table cards is that they are inexpensive to produce and thus easily discarded when readers scribble their own messages on them or use them as scrap paper.

4. *Bookmarks.* Everyone loves a new bookmark—they disappear quickly from library service counters. Bookmarks represent good advertising opportunities—Internet booksellers routinely include them with pur-

chases. Like posters, bookmarks can be purchased with preprinted preservation messages from a variety of sources. However, they are simple and cheap to reproduce in-house so that they not only include a range of preservation messages (perhaps stressing the incompatibility of food, drink, water, and pets with library materials), but also the library's logo, telephone number, and URL. Aside from any message they may convey, bookmarks can also discourage readers from turning down page corners to mark their places or using damaging objects for this purpose (pencils, rulers).

- **Run preservation campaigns.**

Some libraries designate a preservation week or month during which they provide multiple educational opportunities, show films, distribute literature, and mount exhibits. A special poster or button can be produced for such an occasion.

- **Include a preservation element in the library's photocopying operation.**

Almost every library has self-service photocopiers for public use. Both the type of machine selected and the instruction provided to readers who use the equipment can have a significant impact on the library's preservation program, as readers attempt to make copies from bound volumes that are often heavy and small margined.

1. *Select equipment that does not injure materials being copied.* Photocopiers may be preservation "book-edge" machines (also called flush-edge copiers) or traditional flat-glass equipment. Although book-edge machines may be more costly to rent or purchase, because they permit copying without forcing flat the spine of a tightly bound volume (the book can be opened at a 90-degree rather than a 180-degree angle), they can be worth a great deal to a library's preservation program. (Cradle copiers permit a volume to be copied face up and are very preservation friendly, but they are expensive and not so widely available as other types.)

2. *Make available an adequate number of copiers that are (a) well located in terms of readers' needs and convenience and (b) kept in good working order.* It's human nature: when a reader is in a rush, wants to copy (often from a reference book or bound journal volume that cannot be charged out), and there's no machine available—or perhaps the quality of the copy is faint or splotchy—all but the finest citizens will consider tearing out the needed pages. Many persons will move beyond thinking to doing, rationalizing that their behavior is the library's fault—the library should (a) have more copiers, (b) keep them in better running order, or (c) locate them more conveniently. Unfortunately, the library's most expensive volumes—reference materials and bound journals that do not

circulate—are the most likely targets of mutilation when copier services fail. Only infrequently will the reader who is working under pressure subordinate his or her personal needs to the good of the library and its larger public: this makes a fleet of quality copiers central to the library's preservation program.

3. *Price copies favorably and competitively.* The rationale here is similar to that expressed in number 2 above:

   • If readers feel that the price of a copy is too high (particularly if it is greater than that charged by nearby commercial copy centers), they may mutilate volumes rather than pay what seems to them a usurious price.

   • Accordingly, the library must balance the benefits it gains from copier revenues against potential losses to the collections if copy charges are perceived as too steep.

   • If the library raises the per-page cost, it will be well advised to adopt some scheme (perhaps a reduced cost per page when multiple copies are purchased) that continues to give readers access to the lower rate.

4. *Provide signage near equipment that shows the right way to handle a volume while photocopying from it.*

   • This signage should first show readers how to recognize brittle books—those whose pages are likely to break away from the binding if readers attempt to press them down on a photocopier's surface—and tell them where in the library to take these for assistance (perhaps the circulation or reference desk).

   • A sign should *never* indicate that the reader wishing to copy has no options—that the book may not be copied, period. When the brittle book is in safe hands, a staff member can offer the reader a number of options, depending on the book's condition (staff photocopying, note-taking in a supervised area of the library, access to the material after it has been replaced or reformatted, assistance in identifying the same information in another resource).

   • Signs should incorporate both text and illustrations of the proper way to place a nonbrittle bound volume on a copier (avoid smashing or forcing the spine flat).

• **Monitor materials placed on reserve for preservation needs.**

Reserve collections are common in school and academic libraries. By definition, materials that faculty place on reserve are high-demand items to which an entire class or several classes will need access over the course of the school term.

1. *Staff at the reserve desk, like their colleagues at circulation, should examine items as they are charged out or returned.* They can make notes (perhaps in the item's circulation record) about attention the volume requires at the end of the semester when it is no longer needed for reserve.

2. *Staff must also keep the volumes in the reserve collection in sufficiently good repair so that they can remain in circulation.* Pulling a reserve book and sending it to the bindery or a mending unit is not an option. Instead, staff can be trained to make simple nondamaging repairs so that volumes survive until the end of the term, when their needs can be better and more permanently met.

3. *Staff will route worn and damaged volumes no longer needed for reserve to subject specialists for their evaluation.* Selectors will assess these books in terms of their continuing value to the collections, much as they would any other injured title—but with the added caveat that the title is important enough to have recently been placed on reserve.

- **Assist security staff in monitoring the library's entrance and exit.**

Chapter 2, "The Library Building Manager," assigns to this staff member the job of ensuring that book detection gates work well and that staff with security responsibilities perform their duties effectively. This includes denying admission to unauthorized patrons and checking books and bags when those exiting the library set off security alarms. However, someone in the library must be designated to arbitrate at-the-door security issues when readers protest and the authority of security staff needs augmentation or amelioration (a reader has left his or her ID at home and demands entry to the library; an unaffiliated reader wants to apply for library privileges; materials that have not been charged out set off the library's book detection gates). Often access services staff are assigned this responsibility.

Note   1. Jeanne Drewes and Julie A. Page's book *Promoting Preservation Awareness in Libraries: A Sourcebook for Academic, Public, School, and Special Collections,* Greenwood Library Management Collection (Westport, Conn.: Greenwood, 1997), is an essential tool for planning reader education programs for preservation. It is especially valuable to school and public libraries, whose needs are often ignored.

8

Interlibrary Loan

I n many libraries, interlibrary loan and circulation have the same reporting line. They are often part of an access services unit that also includes stack maintenance, privileges, copy services, and reserves. It is easy to see the relationship between interlibrary loan and circulation, because each unit is in the business of lending materials from the collection, whether to individuals (circulation) or to institutions (interlibrary loan) for use by remote individuals. Today some libraries have refashioned their interlibrary loan unit as document supply or document delivery, because many institutions now obtain some number of journal articles requested by their readers from commercial suppliers rather than interlending partners. However, it is the lending of materials from the library's collection that is of interest here.

• Develop and follow an interlibrary lending policy.

Loan policies are one aspect of any preservation program. The policy should include guidelines that enable staff to determine whether or not a volume may be lent (what is its value to the collection? its physical condition?) and what sort of restrictions might be placed on its use once it reaches the borrowing institution.

- Can it be photocopied?
- Will it be allowed to circulate outside the library?
- Is it to be used only in-house?
- Is it to be used only in-house *and* under supervision?

• Identify materials that need treatment.

This is much the same job assigned to circulation staff: recognize volumes that require repair, rebinding, or reformatting, as well as missing materials that are candidates for reselection. Depending on the degree of damage and the item's value, staff might lend it (perhaps with some restrictions on its use) and make a note in the circulation record that it requires attention when it is returned.

• Protect materials during shipping.

Staff should package materials carefully for shipment. Although quality packaging is not inexpensive and may require more staff time to apply, it is well worth the cost because it ensures that the library's materials arrive in good condition.

1. *Many institutions eschew padded envelopes—or at least those that are thinly lined with bubble plastic or foam.* Instead, staff use sturdy boxes.[1]

2. *Audio- or videotapes must never be packed with shredded materials.* This includes fiber-filled padded envelopes: fibers can easily infiltrate the cassette housing, damaging both the tape and playback equipment alike.

3. *Staff should also keep in mind that someone will open the container at the other end of its trip.* They will wrap items so that the implements used to open packages will not damage them.

• Handle materials carefully during inner-institutional shipping.

Many public and academic libraries have branches. When an interlibrary loan request arrives, staff retrieve the item from the branch location and prepare it for shipping to the borrowing institution. A volume or a reel of microfilm may travel to the main library in a satchel carried by a courier traveling on foot or by bicycle (in the case of a university campus) or in a container placed in a van (within a public or regional library system). Whatever the mode of transport, the item should be well protected en route.

• Make reciprocal packaging agreements with interlending partners.

It is all well and good to get a volume to a borrower in good condition: the second half of this exercise is to ensure that, when the item is returned, the borrower packages it as well as the lender did when it was initially sent. (When a library packages its returns as carefully as it does its loans, this creates the sense of a preservation "community.")

• Choose a safe shipping method.

Identifying a method of shipping that is both safe and economical—choosing among a range of commercial couriers and the U.S. mails—is one of the interlibrary loan staff's greatest challenges. Generally speaking, the less time a package spends in transit, the more likely it will arrive in good condition. In making a decision, the staff will want to consider ease of access to the shipper, pricing, insurance, and the shipper's reputation. The library may also wish to stipulate the shipper that the borrowing institution must use to return the item and whether it is to be insured.

• **Examine items upon their return.**

Interlending staff should carefully inspect returned volumes and other items, contacting the borrower as soon as possible about any injury that seems to have been sustained since they were lent.

Note   1. Anyone who has ordered titles from Internet booksellers knows firsthand the value of good packaging. The growth of this industry has given the public a choice among many different companies and generated highly competitive pricing. The *best* price, however, is not always the *lowest* price if the vendor ships in padded envelopes or folded cardboard mailers instead of using plenty of plastic bubble padding and a sturdy corrugated box. A book that arrives with its corners damaged or its dust jacket crumpled cannot be considered a good value.

9

Reference and Information Services

Although the task of developing a formal program for reader education is assigned to access services, most libraries have substantial amounts of student seating near their reference desks so that reference librarians and other staff are well positioned to give readers the sorts of gentle hints about their physical interactions with books that can make a big difference in the life of the collection. Readers are not employees, and they cannot be forced to attend preservation training sessions. This makes it important to use every opportunity to bring them the preservation message.

• **Ask readers to bring damaged materials to the desk.**

This sort of initiative can be especially useful with children, who often like to assist the library staff. It provides opportunities for staff to talk with readers about how books are injured and to provide some low-key instruction in their care and handling. It is a good way to raise the youthful consciousness about preservation.

• **Make well-informed reselection decisions.**

The reference staff is responsible for shaping the reference collection. Worn, damaged, or fragile materials will present themselves for reselection. Using his or her knowledge of the collection, the librarian will decide whether titles are to be withdrawn, replaced, repaired, or perhaps reformatted, following the guidelines in chapter 3, "Collection Development and Acquisitions."

- **Design the library Web site.**

Although library systems staff may actually create and maintain the site (depending on the skills, interests, and duties of the reference and information services staff), librarians in various units will generate the required content.

- **Instruct readers in the proper handling of library materials.**

There is typically a good deal of seating near the reference desk so that librarians and supporting staff assigned there have an excellent vantage from which to observe readers working with library materials and many opportunities to speak informally with them about the ways in which they are handling the collection. A word to

- a researcher stacking books one atop the other with their pages open,
- a child pulling books off the shelves by their headcaps,
- teenagers unpacking their after-school snacks in the listening room,
- a scholar who is using her pen carelessly, or
- someone forcing a volume open on a photocopier

not only addresses the situation at hand, but also purchases insurance for the future, as readers learn small but important lessons about the care of books and other materials. And, just as a department store sales assistant is trained to ask the customer, "Is there anything else I might show you today?" as she closes the sale, at the end of a reference transaction a librarian might ask a reader, "Could I suggest some approaches to caring for the materials you're borrowing today?"

10

Special Collections and Archival Materials

Many libraries have special or rare book collections, as well as archival materials, photographs, maps, newspapers, and realia. Some libraries (local history collections, for example) consist almost entirely of rare or unique materials. The preservation needs of such collections are compounded by their incredibly diverse physical makeup: it is not uncommon to find parchment (sheep- or goatskin), dozens of different varieties of paper, multiple types of ink, and photographic materials in archival collections. These special materials typically hold exceptional monetary, cultural, or research value to the institution and often to larger parts of society. For all these reasons, they have distinctive preservation needs.

- **Ensure that the library provides special materials with the proper climate and surroundings.**

Climate controls and standards are discussed in chapter 2, "The Library Building Manager." If the library's or archive's environment is a poor one—stacks are not properly cooled or heated; there is no humidity control or filtration system; shelving is inadequate; security is substandard; fire protection is limited—the library may wish to deposit valuable collections elsewhere, until a more appropriate setting can be provided. Certainly no new collections should be solicited or accepted until the institution can provide suitable surroundings for them.

- **Conduct collection condition surveys and seek funds for preservation projects.**

The chapters "The Library Director" and "Collection Development and Acquisitions" discuss the importance of conducting collection condition and preservation needs assessment surveys, then seeking funds to address the needs that are identified. Certainly archival and special collections staff should assess the preservation needs of the materials in their care, then write grant proposals accordingly.

- **Design access policies that provide protection for rare and unique materials.**

Consider the following scenarios.

- A historical society holds an open house, to which only its members are invited. Afterward, two valuable documents that were on display for the evening are discovered to be missing.
- A credentialed scholar works for several days with multiple boxes of materials from a single collection. Several months later when another reader applies to use the same materials, important manuscript letters have disappeared.

Unfortunately, such incidents are not as isolated as one might wish. It is almost impossible to take too much care in documenting the use of special and archival collections, while at the same time striving to balance caution with accessibility and a positive service posture. The following three steps represent a basic minimum.

1. *Interview prospective readers.* Only researchers with genuine scholarly needs should be accorded access to special or rare materials.

2. *Require readers to show identification, and photocopy or record this information.* The institution's records should also include the dates on which a researcher used the facility, as well as the names of collections that were accessed. Readers should also sign the collection's guest register. Under some circumstances, the library or archive might request that a researcher provide letters of introduction or recommendation.

3. *When both copies of documents and originals are available, provide access to originals only for those readers to whom this is a scholarly necessity.* The institution that owns both a great writer's notebooks (written in abraded and fading pencil), as well as microfilm copies of the same materials, will allow the originals to be used only under special and compelling circumstances. For most researchers, the copies will suffice.

- **Establish regulations for the use of special collections and archival materials.**[1]

It is likely that experienced researchers are already aware of the particular needs of special materials. However, readers are most likely to treat rare books and manuscripts with special care when the regulations for their use are clearly defined. The library or archive that develops usage policies and shares these with scholars in advance of providing them access to the collections conveys its own commitment to preserving the collections and invites the researcher to be its partner in this effort.

1. *Give researchers who are admitted to the collections a printed copy of the regulations governing their use, which they read and sign.* Staff should also take time to review the library's or archive's rules with readers, before collections are placed in their hands.

2. *Provide a separate, secure area for readers' coats, backpacks, and bags.* Readers should enter the reading room with as little baggage and extraneous material as possible. At the same time, they should not worry that their personal belongings are vulnerable to theft.

3. *Provide a reading room with a single entrance/exit.* If the space has multiple doors, alarm those that are not intended for use.

4. *Examine library and archival materials both* before *and* after *they are given to readers.* Here, staff have two purposes: assessing (a) the *completeness* and (b) the *condition* of materials.

   - COMPLETENESS: if an item included in a container list seems to be missing, this should be noted before the box is given to a researcher. Similarly, when materials are returned, it is best if staff can conduct checks for completeness before the researcher departs.

   - CONDITION: the idea here is to isolate the cause of any damage to the collections. Staff will note the condition of items before and after giving them to researchers (a torn headcap not mentioned in the item's bibliographic description; a crumpled corner on a manuscript sheet).

5. *Provide readers with pencils and paper.* No researcher should be permitted to use ink of any kind while working with special materials. Providing researchers with pencils gives the institution good control. When the library or archive provides note-taking paper as well, it can also give this paper identifying marks of some sort (perhaps something as simple as holes punched along its margin). This enables staff checking the materials that scholars remove from the reading room easily to spot paper not provided by the institution.

6. *Provide facilities for researchers who use portable notebook computers.* These devices have become so much a part of scholarly life that libraries and archives are well advised to set aside some space with suitable tables and wiring and to provide book snakes or other devices designed to hold pages in place while readers work with them. These researchers may merit additional instructions for handling special materials, because taking notes on a computer often causes readers to interact with materials differently than they would were they taking notes with pencil and paper.

7. *Monitor patrons as they work with special materials.* The reading room should be laid out so that researchers sit facing and in full view of the staff, who can observe them as they work. (Conversely, staff may wish to observe researchers using computers from behind.) Patrons should be discouraged from placing obstacles of any sort (even stacks of books) between themselves and the view of library staff.

8. *Provide researchers with photography, photocopying, and scanning services.* Readers are sure to want copies of some of the items they examine. Rather than permitting them to make these copies themselves, the library or archive will provide such services itself, exercising its own judgment about the most suitable and least damaging techniques. Researchers must understand that producing copies sometimes takes time (perhaps the library uses a professional photographer who is not on staff and comes only periodically). Most institutions employ a fee structure for copy services that ensures cost recovery.

9. *Establish procedures for staff to follow when theft is suspected or damage discovered.* Staff need clear guidelines about what to do when they believe an item may have been stolen from the collections or damaged by a researcher. Are they to confront readers directly? Under what circumstances should they attempt to detain a researcher or call for a security officer? Whatever procedures management elects should include a healthy regard for the staff's safety. They should also be recorded and all staff trained to follow them.

10. *Provide appropriate security for exhibit spaces and storage and backlog areas.* It is not just the cataloged collections that are susceptible to loss. Sometimes materials that are on display or awaiting cataloging are easy and inviting targets.

11. *Select both full-time and part-time special collections staff with care.* Unfortunately, some thefts from valuable collections occur at the hands of library or archives staff. Careful reference checks and close supervision help prevent such losses. Policies governing staff interactions with collections are another necessity.

12. *Control the type and number of keys distributed to staff.* This is an excellent rule for the entire library to follow. A carefully planned key program that equips every member of the staff with a few keys that provide access only to necessary areas of the building makes good sense.

- **Ensure that collections are properly cataloged.**

At first glance, this may seem a curious preservation requirement. However, fragile and valuable materials are subjected to much less irrelevant or random handling when they are completely described and cataloged, enabling staff to go immediately to the items readers require. For example, a collection that spans multiple boxes, includes several formats (correspondence, typescripts, memorabilia, photographs), and contains many cubic feet of material will be poorly served by a catalog record that describes its contents in general terms. For more on cataloging special materials, *see* chapter 6, "Cataloging and Materials Processing."

- **Develop and employ guidelines for exhibiting special materials.**[2]

Most institutions that hold special or archival collections take considerable pride in displaying them. Often gift collections come with the requirement that they be exhibited. Exhibits may also be part of the library's or the parent organization's program of public service and outreach. From time to time, libraries and archives will be approached for loans from their collections by other organizations that are planning exhibits of their own. In any case, the location, design, installation, and transport associated with exhibiting precious collections have distinct preservation implications.

1. *Assess the condition of materials being considered for exhibition.* A library or archive is under no obligation to exhibit every item in its collection. Indeed, it is ethically bound to withhold from display those items that are so fragile they would be negatively affected by the experience. Whenever high-quality copies can be substituted for originals (this is particularly advisable with light-sensitive photographs), staff should consider this alternative.

2. *Keep exhibit cases away from sources of strong light.* These might include windows, skylights, and atria; light meters can help the staff make a precise determination of the level of light striking items on exhibit. Because incandescent lighting is less damaging than fluorescent, it is a better choice for exhibit areas, which are also well served when controls allow light levels to be dimmed. Lights can be shut off completely when the exhibit is not open to the public. Ideally, exhibit lighting will be exterior to the cases themselves (case lighting generates a great deal of heat; it can expose items on display to ultraviolet rays at close range). When cases have their own interior sources of lighting and these cannot be removed or shut off, staff should take care that they are shielded with filters, reducing the harm to materials on display.

3. *Monitor the climate inside exhibit cases.* A closed case represents a tiny, self-contained microenvironment whose qualities can have a devastating effect on the materials inside. Not only must the climate in the room itself be monitored, but also that inside the individual cases. Here, hygrometers and cards that change color to indicate shifts in relative humidity are useful tools. Silica gel (which will absorb excess moisture) may also be placed inside cases.

4. *Prohibit food and drink in exhibit areas.* Accidents can happen—even with the most modern and technologically advanced cases. In one of the nation's finest repositories of rare materials, in the course of a reception in the exhibit area, a glass of red wine was overturned on the glass surface of a flat case. Almost immediately the liquid began to seep through the case's seal and fall on the manuscripts inside. No one could locate the key to the case. Ultimately, the glass had to be broken.

5. *Assign well-trained staff the task of installing exhibits.* Only staff trained to handle special materials and knowledgeable about their needs while on display should install exhibits.

6. *Ensure that the interior finishes of the exhibit case are preservationally sound.*

   - Are the cases lined with nonacidic fabric or other material?
   - Will they or any of their components (rubber seals, for example) emit any substances deleterious to the materials on exhibit?
   - Are case interiors smooth and nonabrasive?
   - Is there any material inside the case that might attract insects or other vermin?

7. *Display materials in a supportive and nondamaging fashion.* Staff will find that book cradles and wedges make essential supports for bound volumes. Single sheets are best mounted and displayed flat. Materials should be unfettered by any sort of bands or other restraints.

8. *Monitor materials that are on exhibit.* Despite everyone's best efforts, items on display may begin to show damage—fading, cracking, buckling—over the course of an exhibit. Staff should regularly check cases for distressed materials so that these can be removed and their needs addressed before damage that is costly or irreparable occurs.

9. *Rotate exhibits regularly.* No item should be left on exhibit for a protracted period of time. (Most experts recommend that materials be removed after four to six weeks of display.) During the period of the exhibit, staff should regularly turn the leaves of books on display, curtailing the amount of light to which any pair of pages is subjected.

- **Set criteria for lending special materials.**

Institutions will lend valuable materials only under special circumstances. They will give particular consideration to the preservation needs of items from their collections that are temporarily placed in the care of another organization.

1. *Develop a written policy on loans.*

   - What sorts of items will the library or archive routinely lend?
   - Are there items it will not lend under any circumstances?

- To what types of organizations will the repository make loans?
- Will it lend for traveling as well as fixed exhibits?
- What are the general conditions of any loan, in terms of transportation, liability, insurance, exhibition, and other factors?

2. *Obtain and examine copies of the prospective borrower's (a) exhibition policy and (b) policy for exhibiting borrowed exhibits.* In advance of any loan the library or archive should familiarize itself with the policies of the prospective borrower, enabling it to make decisions about exceptional conditions it may wish to impose.

3. *Ensure that well-trained staff pack materials for shipping.* Materials that are well packed are also easy to *un*pack and *re*pack. This only makes sense: the recipient is less likely to damage materials accidentally when they have been wrapped so that it is both easy and obvious how they should be unwrapped, then rewrapped at the time of return.

4. *Choose a first-rate and reliable shipper.* When an item is quite valuable, a member of the staff may personally deliver it to the borrowing institution. In other cases, an experienced and qualified shipper with a good reputation may be chosen for the job. If the item is not insured by the lending institution, insurance should be obtained from the shipper.

5. *Lend facsimiles rather than originals, whenever possible.* Not every exhibit merits the loan of a valuable original. The library or archive may go so far as to have facsimiles produced for those items that are frequently requested for exhibit.

6. *Limit the frequency with which any item is lent.* Some degree of wear and tear is inevitably associated with each loan, so that no item should be lent repeatedly. To ensure that this does not happen, each institution should maintain a careful account of each item's loan history.

- **House and treat each item in a manner appropriate to its format, use, and protection.**

Special and archival collections often contain multiple formats—books, manuscript materials, photographs, maps, or newspapers. Providing the proper housing and treatment for each material type is a critical aspect of preserving it.[3] Generally, staff are well advised to take three cautionary steps:

1. *Tailor the container to the format.* Because the range of material types is so great, a "one size fits all" approach to collection housing will not work well in most special collections and archives. Staff should ensure that any enclosure fits its contents closely but not tightly. The idea is to support items so that they do not shift or expand; this prevents the damage that can result when contents knock against the sides of a container as it is handled, reshelved, and so forth. (For more on this topic, *see* chapter 6, "Cataloging and Materials Processing.")

2. *Transfer gift collections from the containers in which they arrive to archivally sound ones.* Acidic boxes or folders may have already damaged gift materials; such damage should be halted as quickly as possible.

3. *Combine collection condition surveys and cataloging with preservation projects.* At the same time staff are conducting collection condition surveys or developing collection guides, they can also rehouse materials in suitable alkaline containers.

Many sources describe in detail the particular housing and preservation needs of formats typically found in special collections and archives. Some of the more complete guides are contained in this book's "Resource Guide and Bibliography," and special collections and archival staff are referred to those sources that address the formats their collections contain. Below appear seven material types often contained in archives and special collections, with some basic comments to guide staff about their needs. Chief among these is nonreactive storage containers. (The needs of bound volumes are addressed in chapter 4, "Circulation and Stack Maintenance.")

1. *Manuscript materials.* These may include personal papers, correspondence, institutional records, and manuscripts of published materials. Typically they are flat sheets, far from homogeneous, and can include a wide range of paper and ink types.

   - House each item in a suitable container, removing injurious clamps, clips, rubber bands, and so forth beforehand. Archival supply companies sell a range of container types. Boxes, folders, files, and envelopes should be made from alkaline materials. Inert polyester material such as Mylar can be used to protect brittle single sheet materials. Items that may be highly acidic should be stored alone in folders or containers of their own until decisions can be made about treating or duplicating them. This prevents their acids from migrating to adjacent materials and damaging them.

   - Employ shelving that is wide enough to support archival boxes, so that boxes do not overhang shelf edges. When this happens, eventually the boxes will sag and their fragile contents will become distorted.

2. *Ephemera.* These materials may include pamphlets, broadsides, clippings, scrapbooks, and posters. The makeup and acidity of the paper on which they are printed can vary enormously.

   - Consult sources that address each item's individual needs before making housing and preservation decisions. (For example, on its Web site, the Library of Congress offers advice on preserving scrapbooks.)[4]

   - Place smaller pieces of ephemera (pamphlets, broadsides) in acid-free or inert polyester folders or sleeves, then into archival boxes. They may be treated very much like the manuscript materials mentioned above.

- Handle posters, depending on their size, much like maps (number 3, below).

- Scrapbooks may be custom boxed. In cases where the paper on which the photographs and other objects have been mounted is highly acidic, the library or archive may wish to consider dismantling the scrapbook and rehousing its individual items.

- Consider microfilming or preservation photocopying for clipping files.

3. *Maps.* Maps come in many sizes. Although most are paper based, some are stiffened or backed with other materials. Levels of acidity vary from map to map. Many of the precautions staff take with flat archival materials are also appropriate to maps.

  - House maps flat and unfolded in individual alkaline or polyester folders placed in purpose-built map cases whose drawers are shallow. Avoid overloading drawers, burying some maps under many others: this only increases the possibility that an individual item will be damaged when it is removed for use.

  - Store maps in rolls only when they are so large no other option is feasible. In such cases, maps may be wrapped around acid-free tubes, then covered with alkaline-buffered paper.

  - Ensure that book pockets containing maps are nonacidic. This may mean replacing the original pocket. Alternatively, maps can be removed, unfolded, and rehoused in an accompanying folder.

  - Provide table space sufficient to open and support large maps.

4. *Photographs.* The physical makeup of photographic materials (and thus the issue of their stability) is even more complex than that of many manuscripts and ephemera. A photograph is typically a three-part composite—a support layer (paper, film, glass, plastic); a binder or emulsion (gelatin, albumen, collodion); and the final image material (silver, color dyes, or pigment particles), usually suspended in the emulsion or binder layer.[5] Staff in charge of photographic collections require special training and will benefit from examining the sources related to photographs contained in this book's "Resource Guide and Bibliography." Photographs are difficult or impossible to repair, which means that vigilance in protecting them is particularly important.

  - Maintain storage conditions that are cooler and dryer than those for the general collection.

  - Evaluate photographic negatives (are they nitrate, cellulose acetate, or polyester?), and store them appropriately. (Most institutions are not equipped to store nitrate negatives and will instead take steps to duplicate the images they contain or transfer them to special storage facilities.)

- Remove photographs mounted on acidic paper or other backings and rehouse them.
- Store photographs in individual archival-quality envelopes away from sources of light. Enclosures might be made from alkaline-buffered acid-free paper or transparent polyester. (When transparent envelopes are used, readers can often work with photographs without removing them. This diminishes the level of handling to which these materials are subjected.)
- House smaller photographs upright in metal file boxes with supportive dividers and nonreactive finishes, larger ones in flat boxes or files.
- House photographs of a similar size together.
- House positives and negatives separately: if calamity befalls one group, the odds are better that the other will survive.
- Consider creating copies of photographs that are frequently consulted.
- Provide light cotton gloves and particular supervision for readers who are working with photographs, whose surfaces should never be touched.

5. *Newspapers.* It is likely that older newspapers are embrittled. They may have been further damaged by binding or wrapping in acidic papers (thought at the time to be protective).

- Obtain microfilms of newspapers the institution wishes to preserve. These may be products of one of the country's several newspaper preservation projects.[6]
- Where such films do not exist, send the papers for microfilming. (If a state filming project exists, perhaps the library can participate.)
- As an adjunct to filming or purchasing films, and if the organization has the space to do so, save original newspapers (those not so brittle that they are destroyed by microfilming), in the event mass treatment approaches become available and affordable before the newsprint completely disintegrates.

6. *Realia.* Many special collections contain objects—a bust or statuette that may be made from wood, plaster, or any one of many metals; globes or three-dimensional models; clothing or furniture. Here, it is imperative that staff consult resources that specifically treat the needs of the item in question. (The Henry Ford Museum and Greenfield Village Web site offers guidance on costume and textile preservation.)[7]

- Keep objects safe from dust.
- Protect them from random touching or handling.
- Cover them or place them in protective containers when they are not on exhibit.

7. *Pictures.* Archives and special collections often include paintings, watercolors, and pictures in other media. Whether or not these have any particular monetary importance, they often represent considerable cultural capital, Works Progress Administration (WPA) murals painted in a studio high atop the library's clock tower, for example.

- Protect pictures from inappropriate handling and storage.
- Guard them against dust and excessive light.
- Inspect pictures for evidence of injury or deterioration, taking corrective steps.

- **Make a record of all treatments applied to an item, including notes on those that must be deferred until a later time.**

1. *Maintain a complete record of every treatment applied to an item (cleaning, washing, deacidification, leaf casting, rebinding), including the date of the treatment and the materials used; this is a critical part of its preservation.* When a book or manuscript begins to show signs of deterioration, such records can provide important information about what has been done in the past—information that may literally save its life. Although the byword of contemporary preservation is *reversibility* (conservators do nothing to an item that cannot be undone), mistakes can happen: treatments that were thought to be palliative may instead prove injurious. When damage occurs, knowledge of solutions, dressings, or other applications that were previously used may indicate the most effective future course of action.

2. *Make records of those treatments that must be deferred until funds and priorities permit.* Gift collections bring with them their own preservation problems. Often, as the result of a collection condition survey, items requiring treatment present themselves. In such cases, if the library's or archive's preservation priorities lie elsewhere or funds will not stretch to address the collection's preservation needs, staff will make careful records of each item's requirements. This enables staff to

- ensure that items' preservation needs are not forgotten, simply because they are not immediately addressed;
- prioritize the collection for treatment, fully aware of its preservation needs; and
- avoid unnecessarily rehandling and reassessing every item at some later date.

- **Seek funds for preservation from collection donors.**

Often staff ask donors, as a part of their gift, to designate funds for organizing a new collection. Similarly, the special collections librarian or archivist should request that each gift include support for a conservation survey and any subsequent treatment or rehousing that survey may suggest. Even better, the library or archive can ask the donor to establish a fund whose interest will support both the conservation and expansion of the collection in perpetuity. This approach is an especially appealing one, because new purchases often bring with them their own conservation needs.

- **Create surrogates for rare and fragile materials, preserving intellectual content and reducing the handling of originals.**

When originals are so fragile that their survival is of concern, staff may take steps to have preservation microfilms or photocopies made. (At the present, digital technologies do not offer the same assurance of longevity as does silver gelatin film or alkaline paper. For more on this, see chapter 11, "Microforms, Sound Recordings, Video Formats, and New Media.")[8]

Service copies of special materials may be created by photographing, microfilming, or scanning or digitizing them. Offering these surrogates to readers significantly reduces the necessity of handling the originals. Scanned materials can be made available on disc or via the Internet; readers comment favorably on the ease of access imaging approaches offer. Whatever reproduction technique the library chooses, and whatever the purpose, staff should ensure that the filmer, photographer, or digitizer adheres to accepted guidelines (such as those of the Library of Congress, the Research Libraries Group, and the National Archives and Records Administration) for permanence, durability, and fidelity. When standards are ignored, at a later date the library may find it necessary to create still another copy of a fragile original that is best handled as infrequently as possible.

- **Arrange for conservation measures when these are necessary.**

Often the preservation needs of special materials are beyond the capabilities of the staff, who are not trained conservators. Indeed, staff should not repair or treat rare or archival materials (actions that, while well intended, may do more harm than good). Their job involves three steps:

1. *Recognize the indicators that an item requires treatment.* Such indicators may include mold, insect damage, brittleness, and broken sewing.

2. *Identify a qualified conservator or conservation service.* Local or regional organizations like the Northeast Document Conservation Center provide an array of treatment services to institutions that do not have in-house conservation staff and laboratories. Staff should identify and assess service centers and the assistance each offers. (Some geographic areas offer more choices than others.) Whether the organization chooses an independent conservator or a service center, it should seek recommendations from other institutions. The chapter "The Library Director" provides more detailed guidance on identifying a preservation consultant or service center.

3. *Arrange to have materials professionally treated.* Recommended treatments might include deacidification, paper washing, leaf casting, resewing, and other conservation approaches.

Notes

1. The Association of College and Research Libraries' "Guidelines for the Security of Rare Books, Manuscripts, and Other Special Collections" [Online], (Chicago: Association of College and Research Libraries, 1999) [cited 5 January 2001]), available at <http://www.ala.org/acrl/guides/raresecu.html>, will be of particular help here.

2. Roberta Pilette's thorough guide to exhibition policy and preparation appears in *Preservation: Issues and Planning*, ed. Paul N. Banks and Roberta Pilette (Chicago: American Library Association, 2000), 185–205.

3. The National Parks Service's Conserve-O-Gram Series [Online], [cited 5 January 2001], available at <http://www.cr.nps.gov/csd/publications/conserveogram/cons_toc.html> offers comprehensive information about preserving and caring for a wide range of special formats, including photographs, paintings, textiles, historic documents, and realia.

4. Barbara Fleisher Zucker, *Preservation of Scrapbooks and Albums* [Online], (Washington, D.C.: Library of Congress, Preservation Directorate, 1998) [cited 5 January 2001]); available at <http://lcweb.loc.gov/preserv/care/scrapbk.html>.

5. Mark Roosa, *Care, Handling, and Storage of Photographs* [Online], (Washington, D.C.: Library of Congress, Preservation Directorate, 1992) [cited 5 January 2001]; available at <http://lcweb.loc.gov/preserv/care/photolea.html>.

6. The United States Newspaper Program, a collaboration between the National Endowment for the Humanities and the Library of Congress, is a good source. Available at <http://www.neh.gov/preservation/usnp.html; http://lcweb.loc.gov/preserv/usnppr.html>.

7. Henry Ford Museum and Greenfield Village, *The Care and Preservation of Antique Textiles and Costumes* [Online], (Dearborn, Mich.: Henry Ford Museum and Greenfield Village, n.d.) [cited 5 January 2001]); available at <http://www.hfmgv.org/histories/cis/textile.html>.

8. Both the Northeast Document Conservation Center <http://www.nedcc.org/calendar.htm> and Cornell University <http://www.library.cornell.edu/preservation/workshop/> offer workshops on understanding preservation issues related to digital imaging.

11

Microforms, Sound Recordings,
Video Formats, and New Media

In most libraries, the largest part of the collection will consist of bound volumes, both monographs and serials. However, many institutions also collect so-called special formats—"unbooks"—microforms, sound recordings, videos, and what we might think of as new media: electronic formats accessed via computer. Certainly, these nonbook formats are gaining on the traditional book in terms of the percentage of the collection each represents. Each requires its own sort of housing, equipment, and care, as well as a collection development policy and a plan for its access and circulation.

A quality library environment is very important for these materials, as they are often particularly sensitive to heat, direct sunlight, humidity, dust, and the black, smudgy particulate matter common to urban environments. Such environmental negatives can lead to shrinking, fading, embrittlement, fungal infections, and even surface flaking or peeling. These formats will profit from the same sort of stable climate recommended for the entire library in chapter 2, "The Library Building Manager." If anything, a somewhat cooler and dryer setting is recommended for nonbook materials, when this can be achieved economically.

The preservation needs of nonbook materials are often more complex and more difficult to meet than those of ink on paper.

- Film and electronic resources are not as durable as the printed page, and they respond more rapidly and negatively to extreme or erratic environmental conditions.

- When deterioration occurs, it is often swift and sweeping (a computer file is suddenly unreadable), whereas books typically experience a more gradual decline.

- Nonbook media cannot be read or heard without the aid of suitable equipment—equipment that is often abrasive and can contribute to their deterioration.

- When either format or equipment becomes outmoded (the wax cylinder and the phonograph that played it, for example), unless the resource has been transferred or migrated to a new medium accessible via a new machine, it is lost.

This chapter and chapter 10, "Special Collections and Archival Materials," consider staff responsibilities related to those nonbook materials most typically found in American libraries. Space considerations constrain the inclusion of every item a library or archive might acquire, and some (particularly older or high-technology formats) are not addressed. Institutions collecting more unusual or complex types of media should consult the literature specific to their collections.

This advice raises the question of *how* a library decides which formats it will acquire. This is an especially important issue in today's world of ceaseless technological change, because new media often require major investments in the equipment needed to access them and have their own distinctive preservation needs. Because nothing should be acquired that cannot be properly preserved and cared for, selectors must consider three elements concerning the role of various formats in the library collection.[1]

1. *Format longevity.* Is it likely that this format (microfilm, CD-ROM) will continue in use for some time?

2. *Equipment cost.* Can the library afford to acquire the equipment (fiche reader, PC) required to access this format?

3. *Reader demand.* The library would be ill-advised to adopt any new circulating format until it knows that those it serves are equipped to use it.

   - Is the library's clientele requesting materials in a particular format? If they are, this probably means that the format is making inroads in the home market—readers are unlikely to ask for movies on DVD unless they themselves own DVD players.[2]

   - If an academic library plans to collect feature-length films on laser disc and the film department is its biggest client for motion pictures, does the film department have access to a laser disc player?

The library must make similar decisions about *retaining* formats it has already begun to collect. For example, few institutions with large collections of sound recordings threw out all their vinyl discs (LPs) with the advent of the compact disc (CD)—rather, they began to collect new recordings as CDs while continuing to provide access to their LP collection (and often still accepting gifts or even making purchases in the older format). So long as the equipment needed to access the older format (turntables, in the case of LPs) is readily available on the market, libraries are safe with a policy of gradual migration, rather than blanket (and costly) replacement.

Microforms

Microfilm is the durable workhorse of nonbook print formats. Properly housed and handled, it will last for many years—and preservation-quality silver halide film will last for hundreds of years.

• Enclose microforms in suitable containers.

This means acid-free envelopes for microfiche and boxes for microfilm. The ties used with rolls of film should also be nonacidic and inert. Rubber bands deteriorate and damage film and are not acceptable under any circumstances.

• Store microforms in sturdy, noninteractive cabinets.

Purpose-built steel cabinets are the library's first choice. The advice about housing for books offered in chapter 2, "The Library Building Manager," applies to microformat cabinets as well.

• Keep microforms clean.

Film is sensitive, and dust or dirt will scratch its surface. Clean storage cabinets contribute to clean film.

• Ensure that reading equipment is clean and well maintained.

Little will damage microfilm as quickly as dirty and decrepit readers or reader-printers. Equipment should be maintained on a regular schedule so that it does not scratch or begrime the film it is designed to read or print.

• Attach use instructions to each piece of reading and printing equipment.

Ease of use is another important preservation feature that microform equipment should possess.

1. *Clearly label each machine with operating instructions.* This will go a long way toward improving readers' success with microform equipment, reducing their aggravation and thus extending the lives of film and fiche. Staff should make certain that the print is large and clear enough to be easily read.

2. *Consider ease of use when evaluating and selecting machines.* Unlike staff, most library readers are not familiar with every piece of equipment's features and operating instructions. Microform machines often seem complicated and hard to manipulate. This can engender frustration that manifests itself through rough treatment of both equipment and film or fiche.

3. *Keep the number of different models to a minimum.* Little is more annoying to a reader than to master one microform machine only to find that the one he or she must use on a subsequent visit operates in a completely different fashion.

- **Encourage readers to handle microforms with care.**

Good instructions for operating microform equipment are just the first step in encouraging readers to handle film and fiche with care. Staff should monitor the microform reading area and offer assistance to those who appear to need it. They can also take the opportunity to show readers the proper way of handling film (hold it by its edges or its leader, rather than getting fingerprints on the surface of the film itself).

- **House microfilm masters separately from print masters and service copies.**

Most microfilms in a library's collection will be commercially produced products. When preservation microfilms are created, however, staff should house master copies in a separate cool and dry environment, away from the service copy that will be used by the public. Some libraries house their preservation masters off-site, at locations specially designed to provide the proper environment for these valuable resources.

Sound Recordings

Many libraries own several different sound-recording formats—LPs, audio-cassettes, and, of course, CDs. Although some formats are digital (CDs) and others magnetic (tape), because they are typically housed in the same unit of the library and cared for by the same staff, they are treated in the same section of this book. Note that the needs of audiotape (whether reel-to-reel or cassette) are very much like those of videotape (reel or cassette)—the physical medium is virtually the same. Similarly, the preservation requirements of audio CDs are like those of CD-ROMs, discussed under "New Media," below.

- **Keep sound recordings clean.**

This is probably the number-one method for preserving sound recordings. Ideally, an LP should be cleaned both before and after it is played, because dirt or dust left on the surface will be ground in when the recording is played, damaging both the sound quality and the surface of the disc. A soft, untreated, and lint-free cotton cloth is the best bet, and cloths made specifically for cleaning LPs can be purchased from library and archival supply companies. Unless a disc is very dirty, it is best to avoid the use of denatured alcohol and other cleaning solutions, as the long-term consequences of liquid cleaners are unclear. Although vinyl discs are certainly more vulnerable to injury than

CDs (which are played by a laser instead of a stylus and possess a more resistant finish), more vigorous approaches to cleaning can injure either format.

• **Maintain playback equipment on a regular basis.**

If the staff could take only one additional precaution beyond keeping sound recordings clean, it should be to maintain the library's playback equipment properly.

1. *Keep CD players, turntables, and audiotape players clean and in good working order.* The disc or tape that has been meticulously housed under perfect climatic conditions can be ruined in moments if it is played on substandard or dirty equipment.

2. *Invest in diamond styli.* They prolong the life of vinyl discs and should be regularly cleaned and replaced according to a schedule. If theft proves to be a problem, they can be charged out to listeners, just as LPs are.

3. *Give special attention to tape players.* When heads become dirty or slip into a state of poor repair, they can abrade, snarl, or mangle the tape inside the cassette.

Libraries with circulating audio collections experience a higher level of complaint about the condition of the collection than is the case with collections that are only available for use in-house, for the following reasons:

• Tapes are often damaged when they are played on substandard or poorly maintained home equipment.

• Vinyl is even more subject to damage, because its surface is more susceptible.

• Listeners may not have top-of-line turntables and syli at home.

• Although CDs are more durable than vinyl or tape, one cannot safely use them to play Frisbee with the dog.

If a library chooses to circulate sound recordings, a certain amount of damage is simply the price of doing business.

• **Consider the viability of a closed-stack policy for sound recordings.**

Without a doubt, a sound-recording collection will fare better and live longer when its contents are paged for listeners, instead of allowing the public to hunt freely among the LPs, discs, or tapes.

• **Favor mediated versus self-service playback.**

If sound recordings can be charged out for home listening, there is probably little point in providing a mediated system for in-house playback: this will not do much to mitigate the damage that inevitably occurs in people's homes. When the collection is a noncirculating one, however, there is considerable benefit in remote playback equipment (so that only staff handle the recordings).

- **Label equipment with instructions on how to operate it and how to handle the collections.**

Just as microform machines should be labeled with operating instructions, so should playback equipment for sound recordings. Suggestions for handling discs and CDs (gently, by their edges, avoiding fingerprints that may cause interruptions in sound delivery) can accompany these directions.

- **Prepare a flyer or broadside about collection care.**

If the collections circulate, a flyer or broadside describing collection care that listeners can take home with them is a good idea. Alternately, staff can affix these instructions to the box, sleeve, or jewel case that houses the recording. Concepts might include handling discs by their edges and suggestions for safely separating a CD from the center hub of its jewel case.

- **Choose containers for audio materials that are consistent with the use the collection will receive.**

LPs, audiotapes, and CDs all come in their own enclosures. Depending on how the library plans to use these media and how heavy their circulation is, staff may opt to leave the items in the sleeves or jewel cases in which they arrive, place them in more durable containers, or transfer them to inert archival-quality containers (a needless expenditure if items are simply going to circulate until they wear out and are junked). Consider these two options for collections where preservation as well as access is a goal:

1. *Rehouse LPs and CDs.* Their original coverings are likely made of acidic board or other material and can be preserved in a separate area.

2. *Substitute high-density polyethylene sleeves for the paper ones manufacturers typically use with LPs.* These are also likely to be acidic.

- **Apply marks of ownership and classification to a sound recording's container rather than the recording itself.**

Labels affixed with adhesive are likely to damage recordings, as the adhesive or inks may eventually bleed through and into the disc itself. Even CDs are vulnerable: the plastic layer atop the data-bearing foil is a thin one, and any damage to it can affect playability.

- **House sound recordings vertically.**

1. *Vinyl LPs are best housed upright on metal shelves with noninteractive finishes.* (*See* chapter 2, "The Library Building Manager.")

   - The shelving's strength—how much weight it will bear—is of critical importance because vinyl discs in quantity are deceptively heavy, weighing perhaps thirty to fifty pounds per linear foot of shelving.

- LPs must be well supported with tall dividers and not packed too tightly on the shelves: otherwise, they will warp or sag in short order.
- The dividers should be frequently interspersed among the items in the collection: recordings must not support each other.

2. *Audiotapes and CDs may be placed in steel cabinets with nonreactive finishes.*
   - In the case of tapes (and all magnetic media), metal housing should also be grounded.
   - Cassettes should be housed upright on their edges, with the section containing the tape at the bottom. (Tape can slip from the reels around which it is wrapped when its carrier is laid flat.)
   - Cassettes that are to be stored without being played for some period of time should be periodically and slowly rewound. (Estimates for frequency of treatment range from three to ten years!)

Video Formats

A library may own a variety of moving-image materials—videocassettes, laser discs, and DVDs. Almost every reader's home will have a VCR (an important consideration for libraries with circulating video collections). Increasing numbers will own DVD players (built into the family PC, if not freestanding). There will probably be little demand for circulating reel film or laser discs. Despite its superior resolution, the laser disc has not swept the home entertainment market as did its cousin the videotape, and libraries with collections of videodiscs are probably those with serious motion-picture collections. Before long, the laser disc's powerful pint-sized sibling, the high-capacity DVD, will likely capture both the home and academic markets. In short, we live in a time of rapidly changing consumer (and thus library) behavior. And even DVD has its competitors, among them VOD (video on demand).

Staff will care for videocassettes, laser discs, and DVDs in the fashion described above for audio materials in like formats. Libraries that own films housed on reels may shelve vertically those that are 16 mm or narrower. Films 35 mm and wider, and large, heavy reels of any width, may be stored flat, stacked no more than three or four canisters high. (This allows the gases that film naturally emits easy escape.)

New Media

Digital media include both materials that began their lives in digital formats (Web e-zines; published multimedia resources that include sound, images, motion, text, and data), as well as those converted from traditional to digital formats (journal backruns; an institution's archival collections; rare books). Digital materials (CD-ROMs and Web resources are among the most common formats) have become incredibly successful owing to the unprecedented levels of access and convenience they provide for readers. As their costs continue to decline, their popularity can only increase, so that libraries must treat seriously related preservation issues.

At the same time, the preservation of digital media (and the staff's responsibility for it) differs substantially from that of all other media, chiefly for three reasons:

1. *Issues of format and hardware obsolescence.*[3] Digital media, the software and equipment needed to access their contents, are changing rapidly. (Today, for example, few libraries own PCs with 5.25-inch floppy drives.) There is every reason to expect that this state of transformation will continue and accelerate. In an environment of spinning technological evolution, the only viable approach to preserving digital information is to migrate it to each new pairing of format and equipment—a task far beyond the expertise and resources of any individual library.

2. *The fragile, ephemeral, and unique nature of digital media.*
   - The carriers of digital information—magnetic tape, CD-ROMs—lack the longevity of alkaline paper and silver halide microfilm.[4]
   - Web sites are born and then die with alarming regularity.[5]
   - Many digital resources have no print equivalent: it is impossible to employ the carriers of whose long lives we are assured (alkaline paper, silver halide film) to preserve a resource that is interactive and may include moving images and sound.
   - Digital media can be altered more easily and less obviously than other information carriers (paper, microfilm), adding the issue of *authenticity*—is this document really what it claims to be?—to the mix of other concerns.

3. *Differences in sales and distribution models.* Many digital products are *leased*, not *purchased* in the way that libraries have always bought and owned outright books, journals, sound recordings, microforms, and so forth.
   - One CD-ROM is returned to the publisher when the next updated one appears.
   - Publishers *lease* access to the information contained in the suites of journals they vend to libraries via the Web.[6] When the locus of ownership shifts, so does the locus for preservation responsibility: a library cannot preserve what it does not own—especially when resources are located on servers at a great distance from the subscribing institution.

For all these reasons, the staff's concern with digital resources will center more on *access* than *preservation.*[7]

• Treat CD-ROMs as audio compact discs are treated.

CD-ROMs have become a very popular format for public and school libraries, in part because the majority of these multimedia titles are aimed at the K–12 market. Most home PCs have CD-ROM drives, so libraries often circulate these items. CD-ROMs may be cleaned, housed, and cared for like CD sound recordings.

Some monographs are published with accompanying CDs. The circulating CD-ROM may be kept on file at the circulation desk and placed in an alkaline paper pocket inside the book when a reader charges it out.

• Back up computer files.

When the library has valuable information resources in computer files, these should be part of a regular backup routine, either on a local PC or a network. Both tape and CD backup systems are available.

• Migrate computer files to new carriers as these appear.

Here, there can be no clearer example than the 5.25-inch floppy, which has been gradually superseded by the 3.5-inch disk. For a time, PCs were routinely available with both 5.25- and 3.5-inch drives. Today, no popular manufacturer makes the larger drive, yet many people were likely caught unaware with data on 5.25-inch disks that they never got around to migrating. (With some luck, their data were not entirely lost because they also reside on a computer hard drive.)

• Show caution in caring for and maintaining floppy disks.

Diamonds may be forever, but disks are not. Floppy disks (today, 3.5 inches) have indeterminate life spans; eventually, they are likely to become corrupted. Despite the existence of good repair and recovery software, some or all of the data a disk contains may become lost or inaccessible. Protect floppies by housing them in dust-free disk boxes, away from food and drink. Transfer data from old or suspect disks to a hard drive or a new floppy, and discard the original disks. Staff should always employ regular backup routines.

• Make use of antivirus software.

Computer viruses can destroy files and data: installing quality antivirus software on all machines in the library helps protect against such disasters.

Notes

1. Perhaps nothing illustrates more powerfully that librarians must be aware of the implications of format shifts than the late-twentieth-century transition in sound-recording formats. Even though CDs seem quite high tech today, they, too, are certain to be replaced in a trend that is unlikely to end.

2. DVD (digital versatile disc or digital videodisc, depending on whose definition one accepts) has a far greater capacity than a videotape or laser disc (one DVD can easily hold two full-length motion pictures), as well as superior resolution and audio.

3. This first issue as well as the one that follows is also relevant for audio and video materials.

4. Many experts do not consider this to be a major issue, because digital information's formats and equipment often become obsolete before their carriers begin to deteriorate.

5. In her July 1998 article in *College & Research Libraries*, "The Cyberarchive: A Look at the Storage and Preservation of Web Sites," Carol Casey advances some interesting ideas about preserving Web sites. A key feature of these interactive tools, however, is their links to other Web resources, so at the present it is hard to see how sites can be preserved in any real sense.

6. Publishers often guarantee libraries "perpetual access," either via CD-ROM or the Web, to journals whose content they have leased for a period of time but later canceled. As publishers merge or fail and older backruns lose commercial value, however, it is doubtful that they can deliver on such promises.

7. This is not to suggest that librarians should ignore preservation issues related to digital information, but rather that these issues must be addressed at levels higher than that of the local library. In 1996 the Task Force on the Archiving of Digital Information (created by the Commission on Preservation and Access and the Research Libraries Group) developed recommendations for the formation of a national network of digital archives to ensure the survival of digital information. Since that time, the RLG Working Group on Digital Archiving has done additional work. The RLG Web site is a good source of information <http://www.rlg.org/ArchTF/; http://www.rlg.org/preserv/archpre.html>, as is the Digital Library Federation's site <http://www.clir.org/diglib/dlfhomepage.htm>.

12

Library Systems

How can the staff who manage the library's technical infrastructure and computer systems participate in the preservation program?[1] Surprisingly, in many ways—particularly if the library uses online catalog software capable of generating tailored management reports or has access to someone fluent in the languages of database construction. In many cases, automation can deliver greater productivity, new capabilities, greater access to collections, and increased functionality for the preservation program.

The potential for success is greater when the library chooses to employ standard software with which staff are likely to be familiar. Staff should think twice about building a key application using a package that will make the application difficult to maintain when the programmer moves on to another organization. (Of course, this automation principle applies to all areas of library work, not just preservation.) For much the same reason, it is wise to avoid extensive custom programming. Instead, it makes more sense for staff to explore Web sites dedicated to preservation, with the purpose of identifying existing software solutions adopted by other institutions.[2]

- **Generate management reports that support the preservation program.**

A selector will find reports of different types very useful in planning preservation projects. These are some examples that might be generated using the library's online integrated library system:

- A list of nineteenth-century British imprints shelved in the open stacks that are to be moved to special collections
- A chart showing the growth rate of monographs classed in PN

- A list of journal runs published in the United States between 1850 and 1900
- A list of all folios
- A list of those monographs with the highest circulation during a recent six-month period

- **Create databases that support the preservation program.**

For an institution with an in-house conservation lab, it is easy to envision the enormous benefit of a comprehensive, searchable collection of preservation program information. The systems unit can provide support by building a database capable of tracking all items in the laboratory, permitting staff to record information such as

- which unit sent each item;
- when it arrived;
- what treatments were performed (rebinding, paper washing, leaf casting, deacidification, reformatting);
- who performed them;
- what materials were used;
- the amount of staff time that was expended;
- any treatments that were deferred; and
- when the item was returned to the home unit.

A single database (networked so that authorized staff can access it and add to it from multiple workstations) can support everything from selection for preservation through treatment. Ideally, the records that form the basis for the database will be machine-readable bibliographic records from the library's online catalog. Even in libraries that lack conservation labs (the very institutions at which this book is aimed), a preservation database can be a valuable thing. It could be used to

- manage the bindery operation and
- collect and analyze survey data of various types (collection condition, site, environmental).

- **Publish materials that support the preservation program.**

Public relations is an important aspect of the preservation program. Publications are a valuable tool for raising readers' consciousness about preservation issues and enlisting their assistance in caring for the collection. If the staff in access services (*see* chapter 7) are skilled in desktop publishing, they may be able to produce a range of flyers, bookmarks, table cards, and posters that support the public preservation program. Alternatively, systems staff can provide them with the necessary training, software, and equipment.

- ## Maintain the library catalog.

The integrated library system (consisting of catalog, circulation, acquisitions, and other modules) is one of the preservation program's most valuable tools. Typically, library systems staff have responsibility for maintaining this system.

- The catalog documents the library's collection.
- Its bibliographic records serve as the basis for preservation surveys and databases.
- It is vital for assessing loss and making replacement decisions if disaster strikes.
- The catalog also provides information about the temporary locations of items removed from the stacks for treatment or reformatting.

- ## Develop and maintain the library Web site.

Preservation initiatives and related documents should have a home on the library's Web site. Systems staff will probably create and maintain the site (depending on the skills, interests, and duties of the reference and information services staff), and librarians in various units will generate the required content.[3] The library Web site will be a team effort. What sorts of preservation information might it carry?

1. *Staff education.* Rudimentary instruction needed by staff in all library units—how to handle various formats, how to remove books from shelves—can appear on the library Web site.

2. *Reader education.* Someone recently commented that, if people spend X hours each day browsing the Web (and for the young, X is a surprisingly high number), libraries had better position themselves to take advantage of this behavioral trend. This means setting the library's Web site as the home page on every machine in the building and then providing readers with useful information that is easy to navigate and attractively presented. Reader education for preservation should be included in this mix. Additionally, the exhibits associated with any preservation campaign can also be translated for the Web and mounted there as virtual exhibits.[4]

3. *Preservation documents.* These might include the library's emergency preparedness and recovery plan and its collection retention plan.

Systems staff should also offer to add relevant information to the Web sites of the library's preservation partners. If the parent organization's security or facilities management units have their own sites, the library's emergency manual should find its way there—or at least the what-to-do, whom-to-call, emergency-supplies-are-located-here parts of the manual.

• **Support a general software application suite.**

All units in the library, whatever their responsibilities, can benefit from training and support in an office applications software suite that includes word-processing, spreadsheet, graphics, desktop-publishing, database, and presentation applications. Among the ways such software can be used in the preservation program is writing reports, creating forms, generating publications, making labels for enclosures, and conducting sampling for preservation needs assessment surveys.

• **Support specialized preservation-related software.**

Specialized software programs may be useful to the preservation program, and systems staff can install and support such programs. These are mentioned in the appropriate chapters of this book. Examples include collection condition software such as Calipr and ABLE bindery preparation software.[5]

• **Provide consultation and support for a variety of computer-assisted projects.**

Staff in the library systems unit can also consult on and provide support for digitization projects (perhaps for archival or photographic collections), the use of laptops for preservation needs surveys, and other special preservation needs.

Notes

1. Alternatively, if the library has no in-house systems staff of its own, the parent organization's systems unit can be asked to support the preservation program in the ways outlined in this chapter.

2. Many commercial software packages can be used in preservation programs for word processing, constructing surveys, building databases, managing image collections, tracking projects, and building spreadsheets.

3. Examples of library Web sites with preservation elements can be found on the Conservation OnLine (CoOL) Resources for Conservation Professionals Web site, at <http://palimpsest.stanford.edu/byorg/deptpg.html>.

4. The Brooklyn College Library's Web site includes interesting virtual exhibits, prepared by assistant archivist Marianne Labatto, at <http://academic.brooklyn.cuny.edu/library/>.

5. Find Calipr: Preservation Planning Software at <http://sunsite.berkeley.edu/CALIPR/>; and ABLE Library Binding Preparation System at <http://www.programmingconcepts.com/able/>.

Resource Guide
and Bibliography

Resource Guide

This book presents a blueprint for designing a preservation program without the presence of a preservationist on staff. The text outlines preventative measures that can be initiated by any library or archive to extend the life of the materials in its collection. Just as importantly, it points out when it is best to turn to the experts. This resource guide is an annotated compilation of organizations that provide preservation assistance as well as referrals to professionals who can help in a variety of ways.

In the fields of preservation and conservation, there is a spectacular network of governmental and private agencies that help both individuals and institutions. For those hoping to start a preservation program, many of these organizations' Web sites offer easy-to-follow instructions, referrals, publications, and specifications for equipment and supplies that are freely available for downloading. Frequent updating is one of the hallmarks of the field, and librarians should check their favorite sites regularly.

Again, Web sites sometimes change their addresses. A keyword search using a favorite engine should help in such cases. Where organizations have made phone numbers and e-mail addresses available, these have been included.

Associations

American Library Association. Association for Library Collections and Technical Services. Preservation and Reformatting Section. 50 E. Huron St., Chicago, IL 60611. (800) 545-2433. E-mail: ala@ala.org. <http://www.ala.org/alcts/organization/pars/index.html>

The Preservation and Reformatting Section (PARS) is composed of nine committees and ten discussion groups. The aim of this section is "to provide leadership in the application of new technologies to assure continued access to library collections." To that end, the groups hold meetings at the American Library Association's (ALA) Midwinter Meeting, put on programs at the Annual Conference, and issue policies and guidelines that articulate ALA's position on preservation. These papers appear on the PARS Web site.

Association of Research Libraries. Preservation Program. 21 Dupont Cir., Ste. 800, Washington, DC 20036. (202) 872-0884.
<http://www.arl.org/preserv/>

The Association of Research Libraries (ARL) is a nonprofit member organization representing the leading research libraries in North America. ARL engages in a variety of programs that benefit its members, including its preservation program, whose objective is to "support member libraries' efforts to preserve research collections, both individually and in the aggregate." To that end ARL issues publications, conducts surveys, engages in a range of projects, and sponsors symposia.

Digital Library Federation. 1755 Massachusetts Ave. NW, Ste. 500, Washington, DC 20036. (202) 939-4750. E-mail: dlf@clir.org.
<http://www.clir.org/diglib/>

The Federation operates under the aegis of the Council on Library and Information Resources (CLIR). A group of research libraries, its goal is to maintain, expand, and preserve a distributed collection of digital materials. In its commitment to long-term access to the digital record, the Federation sponsors research in the preservation of digital film, video, and audio; the cost of digital preservation; and the value of the digital record. The Digital Library Federation publishes on various aspects of preserving digital journals, including migration and emulation.

Research Libraries Group Preservation Program (PRESERV). 1200 Villa St., Mountain View, CA 94041-1100. <http://www.rlg.org/preserv/>

The Research Libraries Group (RLG) is a membership organization consisting of more than 160 cultural institutions. PRESERV, a member activity, is a collaborative effort to preserve and improve access to research materials. For the past twenty years, the Program has played a pivotal role in establishing guidelines for creating and storing micro-film. Recently, PRESERV has turned its attention to accomplishing the same goal for documents both "born-digital" and "born-again digital." To that end, RLG is engaged in a joint project with OCLC to develop a digital-archiving model suitable for large-scale heteroge-neous collections.

Society of American Archivists. 527 S. Wells St., 5th Fl., Chicago, IL 60607-3922. (312) 922-0140. E-mail: info@archivists.org. <http://www.archivists.org/>

> The Society of American Archivists (SAA) provides many opportunities for archivists to share their expertise and professional interests. This association establishes standards for archival certification and each year offers numerous workshops, held at various sites around the country. SAA holds an annual conference and acts as publisher or distributor for more than one hundred titles, including the *American Archivist and Archival Outlook*. The SAA Web site gives a brief history of the archival profession from its genesis to the present day. SAA's Preservation Section has its own site, <http://dlis.gseis.ucla.edu/saap-reserv/prindex.htm>, maintained by the University of California at Los Angeles's Department of Library and Information Science. This site includes the Preservation Section's newsletters, a bibliography, and links to other preservation Web sites.

Businesses

Acme Bookbinding. P.O. Box 290699, 100 Cambridge St., Charlestown, MA 02129-0212. <http://www.acmebook.com/>

> This family-run company, founded in 1821, supplies bindery, preservation, and digitization services. Acme builds phase boxes to order and also offers the ABLE binding preparation software (covered in the "Binding" section of the bibliography).

Eastman Kodak Company. <http://www.kodak.com>

> From its Web site, Kodak offers a wealth of current information about the care, storage, and preservation of photographs and film.

Gaylord Brothers. P.O. Box 4901, Syracuse, NY 13221-4901. Customer service: (800) 634-6307. E-mail: needham@gaylord.com. <http://www.archival.gaylord.com/>

> Gaylord sells archival supplies (including enclosures), distributes its own free archival publications (which can be downloaded from the Web), and provides gratis kits that can be used with preservation workshops. This firm also offers archival help via e-mail and takes questions by telephone two days a week. Its Web site includes both "technical tips" and frequently asked questions.

ProText, Inc. 3515 Leland St., Bethesda, MD 20815. (301) 718-1659. E-mail: protext@protext.net. <http://www.protext.net>

> This company sells products, provides referrals, and distributes information on disaster preparation and recovery. ProText's Web site lists

independent contractors and organizations that provide advice and also lists companies that engage in salvage operations. One of their products, the REACT PAK, is described as a first-aid kit for disaster recovery. It includes their RESCUBE, a reusable polyethylene corrugated box for packing damaged books that can withstand extremely cold temperatures.

Talas. 568 Broadway, New York, NY 10012. (212) 219-0770.
E-mail: info@talasonline.com. <http://talas-nyc.com>

This company stocks an extensive array of preservation, conservation, and restoration supplies. Its Web site contains an international database of conservators and bookbinders that is sorted into fifteen categories, including archaeological objects and electronic materials.

Emergency Preparedness and Recovery

The preservation field service centers listed in the "Regional Conservation Centers and Field Services" section, below, address the issue of physical disasters in cultural institutions. At a minimum, these organizations provide training and instructional materials that detail what the stricken institution should do before, during, and after an emergency. The "Emergency Planning" section in the bibliography also provides guidance in this area. (Karen E. Brown's *Worksheet for Outlining a Disaster Plan* and the ProText and SOLINET Web sites list businesses dedicated to one or more aspects of planning or recovery.)

The field service centers also offer telephone consultation, and some will send trained people to the disaster site. Here are a few examples of firms and consultants who offer disaster assistance. Inclusion does not constitute an endorsement or a recommendation over an entity that is not listed. Many companies in this field change their addresses frequently and have numerous offices in different regions.

American Freeze-Dry, Inc. 411 White Horse Pike, Audubon, NJ 08106.
(609) 546-0777.

Disaster recovery services

Chicora Foundation, Inc. P.O. Box 8664, Columbia, SC 29202.
(803) 787-6910. E-mail: information@chicora.org. <http://www.
chicora.org/>

Pest control, environmental consulting, architectural consulting

Document Reprocessors
San Francisco Office, 1384 Rollins Rd., Burlingame, CA 94010. (800) 437-9464, 24 hours; (650) 401-7711.
<http://www.documentreprocessors.com/frames.html>

New York Office, 5611 Water St., Middlesex, NY 14507. (800) 437-9464, 24 hours; (716) 554-4500.

> Vacuum freeze-drying; smoke removal, cleaning, fumigation; mobile drying chambers for on-site treatment

MBK Consulting. 60 N. Harding Rd., Columbus, OH 43209-1524.

> Consulting, information

Munters Moisture Control Services. Central Office, P.O. Box 640, Amesbury, MA 01913. (978) 388-4900.

> Disaster recovery, dehumidification, vacuum freeze-drying, mold removal

ProText, Inc. 3515 Leland St., Bethesda, MD 20815. (301) 718-1659. E-mail: protext@protext.net. <http://www.protext.net>

> Emergency response kits

Funding Agencies

Funding Resources for Preservation. <http://palimpsest.stanford.edu/solinet/fundres.htm>

> This leaflet describes national, public, and private funding agencies and state funding agencies in the southeastern United States.

The Institute of Museum and Library Services. 1100 Pennsylvania Ave. NW, Washington, DC 20506. (202) 606-8536. E-mail: imlsinfo@imls.gov. <http://www.imls.gov/>

> The Institute of Museum and Library Services (IMLS) is a significant source of funding for conservation projects. An independent agency, it was created by the Museum and Library Services Act of 1996. The legislation provides for funding through 2002. For fiscal year 1999, $166.2 million was earmarked for the library program and $23.4 million for museums. The legislation apportions at least 91.5 percent of the library funds via state library agencies for a number of initiatives. Three of these are the Conservation Assessment Program, Conservation Project Support, and National Leadership Grants for Libraries. The Web site provides details on every grant funded with monies from IMLS since its inception, as well as guidelines and deadlines for applying for upcoming grants.

National Endowment for the Humanities. Division of Preservation and Access. 1100 Pennsylvania Ave. NW, Washington, DC 20506. (202) 606-8400. E-mail: info@neh.gov. <http://www.neh.fed.us/preservation/index.html>

> The National Endowment for the Humanities (NEH) is the largest source of funding for humanities programs in the United States. The

Division of Preservation and Access supports one of the four initiatives of the endowment, preserving and providing access to cultural resources. It achieves this goal through grants for the safeguarding of collections, reformatting brittle books, supporting the U.S. Newspaper Program (described in the bibliography), and educational programs. More than $132 billion has been generated from the challenge grants and matching funds alone.

National Historical Publications and Records Commission. National Archives and Records Administration. 700 Pennsylvania Ave. NW, Rm. 111, Washington, DC 20408-0001. (202) 501-5610. E-mail: nhprc@arch1.nara.gov. <http://www.nara.gov/nhprc/>

This Web site contains the work of the National Historical Publications and Records Commission (NHPRC), which gives grants to individuals and institutions that "preserve, publish, and encourage the use of documentary sources relating to the history of the United States." The commission will receive up to $10 million for the fiscal year 2001. The site gives information about previously funded grants, directions for how to apply, and deadlines.

Organizations

American Institute for Conservation of Historic and Artistic Works. 1717 K St. NW, Washington, DC 20006. E-mail: info@aic-faic.org. <http://aic.stanford.edu/>

The American Institute for Conservation of Historic and Artistic Works (AIC) is dedicated to the profession of conservation, which it defines as the preservation and restoration of cultural property. Those interested in conservation are invited to join the organization at a variety of levels. AIC holds an annual national conference, provides financial assistance for professional development, and has a code of ethics that its members are expected to follow. On the Web site one can find definitions of conservation terminology, descriptions of conservation specialties, instructions on caring for treasures, requirements for becoming a conservator, resources on health and safety, and links to related sites. AIC also provides guidelines for selecting a conservator. As part of this service, the institute will recommend candidates from its membership rolls.

The Center for Book Arts. 28 W. 27th St., New York, NY 10001. (212) 481-0295. E-mail: info@centerforbookarts.org. <http://centerforbookarts.org/>

The Center is a nonprofit organization committed to advancing the craft of what it calls bookmaking and to promoting the concept of the book as an art form. To that end, it mounts exhibits, assists book artists, and acts as publisher or distributor for a number of publications, including its own exhibition catalogs. The Center offers a dazzling array of courses, workshops, and seminars at all levels of expertise including those on printing, binding, paper marbling, and simple book repair. Those who enroll can also learn to make photo albums, Christmas cards, invitations, or business cards. A "how-to" Web page, which will offer online instruction and a discussion forum, is being developed.

Council on Library and Information Resources. 1755 Massachusetts Ave. NW, Ste. 500, Washington, DC 20036. (202) 939-4750. E-mail: info@clir.org. <http://www.clir.org/>

> Formed in 1955 as the Council on Library Resources, CLR led to the creation of the Commission on Preservation and Access in 1988. In 1997, these organizations merged under the present name. The Council collaborates with many agencies to serve as a forum for change. It promotes traditional preservation solutions such as microfilming and environmental controls and also marshals experts to evaluate innovative solutions to preservation problems. Among CLIR's research interests are mass deacidification and structures for digital archives. CLIR is the administrative arm of the Digital Library Federation (reviewed in this guide). The Council publishes newsletters, technical reports, and research briefs, many of which are available on its Web site within weeks of issuance. One such set of documents is *Guides to Quality in Visual Resource Imaging*, a series of five guides issued jointly by CLIR and the Research Libraries Group.

Dartmouth College Preservation Services. Hanover, NH 03755. (603) 646-1110. E-mail: preservation.services@dartmouth.edu. <http://www.dartmouth.edu/~preserve/>

> This comprehensive site gives practical information geared to staff without preservation expertise. It includes a detailed instruction guide called *A Simple Book Repair Manual*, funded by the National Park Service's National Center for Preservation Technology and Training, as well as a treatment section, frequently asked questions, and directions for what to do when an emergency threatens the collection.

Image Permanence Institute. Rochester Institute of Technology. 70 Lomb Memorial Dr., Rochester, NY 14623. (716) 474-5199. <http://www.rit.edu/~661www1/>

> This unique laboratory focuses on research into visual and related forms of the cultural record. Two of the Image Permanence Institute's (IPI's) inventions are PAT (Photographic Activity Test), which meets international standards for determining the archival quality of enclosures, and A-D strips, which measure the severity of acetate film deterioration (vinegar syndrome). IPI also provides training and consulting services.

Library of Congress. *Preservation*. Washington, DC 20540-4500. (202) 707-5213. E-mail: preserve@loc.gov. <http://lcweb.loc.gov/preserv/>

> This Web site presents the activities of the Preservation Directorate, whose purpose is to preserve Library of Congress (LC) collections. The directorate assumes a leadership role in educating the public about how best to preserve and conserve library and personal collections. The site includes a number of instructional leaflets detailing the care of every type of material found in library collections and several pages devoted to cutting-edge conservation methods currently in use at LC. There is also guidance on disaster mitigation and a list of LC's specifications for preservation supplies (paper, card stock, mat board, and labels). The site gives information on LC's annual preservation workshop (referred to in the "Workshop" section of this guide), as well as information about conservation fellowships and internships. There is a section of frequently asked questions.

National Archives and Record Administration. *Archives and Preservation Resources*. 700 Pennsylvania Ave. NW, Washington, DC 20408. E-mail: preserve@nara.gov. <http://www.nara.gov/arch>

> The National Archives and Record Administration (NARA) is an independent federal agency that oversees the management of all federal records as well as all presidential papers since the time of Herbert Hoover. NARA's Web site provides guidance on archival preservation at all levels, from that suited to the at-home record keeper to advice for professionals. Included are the Archivist's Code (1955), an explanation of training requirements for archivists, and definitions of preservation and conservation as they relate to federal records. NARA offers workshops and conferences for archivists and other professionals. Its Web site also includes full-text documents on arranging, storing, and reformatting records, as well as disaster preparedness for archival materials.

Preservation Resources, a division of OCLC Online Computer Library Center. 9 S. Commerce Way, Bethlehem, PA 18017-8916. (610) 758-8700. E-mail: presres@oclc.org. <http://www.oclc.org/oclc/presres/>

> This organization purports to be the only one in the United States devoted exclusively to providing quality preservation reformatting services to the educational community. It microfilms books, documents, and photographs and supplies a full array of pre- and postmicrofilming services, including digital scanning. Preservation Resources also offers professional consultation and workshops.

Regional Conservation Centers and Field Services

Regional conservation centers perform a variety of functions, serving cultural institutions that may not have their own conservation facilities. Staff at such centers often perform collection surveys, facilitate collection assessments, provide emergency assistance, treat books and other objects, deliver seminars, and organize workshops. Many centers belong to the Association of Regional Conservation Centers (ARCC); information about ARCC and its members can be found at <http://www.rap-arcc.org/>. This site also provides educational leaflets and a starter kit for collection managers.

Amigos Library Services. 14400 Midway Rd., Dallas, TX 75244-3509. (972) 851-8000; (800) 843-8482. E-mail: amigos@amigos.org. <http://www.amigos.org/preserve.htm>

> Amigos offers different types of aid to libraries and other cultural institutions in the southwestern United States, primarily in the states of Arizona, Arkansas, New Mexico, Oklahoma, and Texas. Staff provide disaster recovery assistance, training through workshops and presentations, site surveys, and telephone reference and referrals. On the Amigos Web site, linked to "informational handouts," are resources on preservation with particular emphasis on book repair, emergencies, and replacements. The site also offers topically arranged bibliographies, videographies, and archival material suppliers, as well as guidelines for selecting preservation supplies and a sample disaster plan.

The Conservation Center for Art and Historic Artifacts. 264 S. 23d St., Philadelphia, PA 19103. (215) 545-0613. E-mail: ccaha@ccaha.org. <http://www.ccaha.org>

> The Conservation Center for Art and Historic Artifacts (CCAHA), founded in 1977, is one of the largest regional conservation centers in the United States. Its services are available to public and private institutions, as well as individuals. In its state-of-the-art laboratory, the Center specializes in the treatment of art and artifacts on paper, such as drawings, maps, historic wallpaper, scores, photographs, and manuscripts. Parchment and papyrus are also treated. CCAHA provides on-site consultation surveys, preservation planning, workshops, grant assistance, and on-site emergency assistance.

Northeast Document Conservation Center. 100 Brickstone Square, Andover, MA 01810-1494. (978) 470-1010. E-mail: nedcc@nedcc.org. <http://www.nedcc.org/>

> The Northeast Document Conservation Center (NEDCC) is the largest regional conservation center in the United States. Founded in 1973, it provides a vast array of services to libraries, other cultural institutions, and individuals—this is truly "one-stop shopping." The Center has four departments: Field Services, Paper Conservation, Book Conservation, and Reprographic Services. The Field Services Office, supported by the National Endowment for the Humanities, provides without charge telephone assistance for disaster relief (24/7) and conservation advice. Staff

offer workshops and seminars, the invaluable manual *Preservation of Library and Archival Materials* (*see* the bibliography), preservation surveys, and assistance with grant applications. The Book and Paper Conservation Departments perform a variety of conservation services in their state-of-the-art labs. Reprographics Services offers preservation microfilming and the duplication of photographs. The NEDCC Web site links to granting agencies and includes frequently asked questions and links to the technical leaflets in the *Preservation of Library and Archival Materials* manual.

Northern States Conservation Center. P.O. Box 8081, St. Paul, MN 55108. (612) 378-9379. E-mail: altenhuber@wavetech.net. <http://www.collectioncare.org/>

The Northern States Conservation Center (NSCC) offers conservation treatment for three-dimensional objects, works of art on paper, sculpture, furniture, and photographs. It serves museums and other cultural institutions by training and consulting on environmental issues as well as treatment. The NSCC Web site "Collection Care" incorporates full-text articles, an annotated list of its conservation book collection, tips on general collection care, descriptions of unusual implements for care and disaster mitigation, information on workshops, grant-writing assistance, and sources of funding.

SOLINET Preservation Services. 1438 W. Peachtree St. NW, Ste. 200, Atlanta, GA 30309-2955. (404) 892-0943. <http://www.solinet.net/presvtn/preshome.htm>

Preservation Services is an arm of SOLINET (Southeastern Library Network, Inc.). With more than 800 member libraries, SOLINET is the largest regional library network in the United States, serving Alabama, Florida, Georgia, Kentucky, Louisiana, Mississippi, North Carolina, South Carolina, Tennessee, Virginia, and the Caribbean. Preservation Services, supported in part by NEH, extends assistance under the auspices of two programs: the Microfilm Service, which to date has preserved the intellectual content of more than 86,000 brittle volumes, and Field Services, the oldest such program in a bibliographic network. Field Services provides workshops, free leaflets, publications, a free information and referral service, an audiovisual loan service, and a consulting service. On the Web site are full-text leaflets, descriptions of SOLINET publications, links to related sites, a "What's New" page, frequently asked questions, and a list of disaster recovery services and supplies.

Upper Midwest Conservation Association. 2400 Third Ave., South Minneapolis, MN 55404. (612) 870-3120. E-mail: umca@aol.com. <http://www.preserveart.org/>

This organization is an art conservation treatment center for works owned by either institutions or individuals. Member institutions pay a nominal fee, which gives them discounts and priority service. The Field Services Department, subsidized by NEH, conducts surveys using a sliding scale of fees so that any institution can afford this service. Technical advice is available free of charge by telephone, fax, and in writing. Salvage assistance is offered around the clock through telephone consultations, and emergency preparedness planning is provided by telephone, workshop, and on-site consultations.

Supplies

Many companies sell preservation, conservation, and disaster mitigation supplies. At the end of each leaflet in Ogden's *Preservation of Library and Archival Materials: A Manual* (eleven of these are included in the bibliography) is a list of firms whose merchandise is pertinent to the topic addressed. Additionally, the Amigos <http://www.amigos.org/> and CoOL <http://palimpsest. stanford.edu> Web sites include many such companies, arranged by the type of materials in which they specialize. At LC's Web site, <http://lcweb. loc.gov/preserv/>, is a description of the preservation products that they use and their specifications for these items. Many of the companies listed in the "Businesses" section also sell supplies.

Workshops

In any given year, many institutions hold preservation workshops. To learn more about what is available, check with the nearest regional library center, regional conservation center, or the preservation department of a local library school. Many of the associations and organizations listed in this guide also hold workshops. These are examples of institutions that hold preservation workshops and their recent offerings.

Cornell University Libraries. "Moving Theory into Practice: Digital Imaging for Libraries and Archives." [Workshop]. <http://www.library. cornell.edu/preservation/workshop/>

> This is a five-day workshop being offered seven times over a period of two years and largely subsidized by NEH.

Library of Congress. "Preservation Awareness Workshops." [Workshop series]. <http://lcweb.loc.gov/preserv/aware.html>

> LC holds an annual workshop cosponsored by the Library's Center for the Book and its Preservation Directorate. The workshop is part of the celebration of National Library Week in April.

Northeast Document Conservation Center. "Workshops/Seminars." [Workshop series]. <http://www.nedcc.org/calendar.htm>

> NEDCC's workshops are given at various sites throughout New England.

Rutgers, the State University of New Jersey. School of Communication, Information, and Library Studies. Preservation Management Institute. <http://www.scils.rutgers.edu/ac/pds/pmi.jsp>

> The Preservation Management Institute is located at Rutgers University, New Brunswick, New Jersey. Participants who complete the program earn a Certificate in Preservation Management from Rutgers. This workshop attracts people from across the United States.

Bibliography

This bibliography contains citations for all items mentioned in the text, as well as citations to additional useful documents. Included are documents that reflect current thinking on preservation techniques, reports from professional organizations working to further the national preservation agenda, and simple preservation instructions. The availability of many of these works in electronic form facilitates their frequent updating and revision. This is especially important in the field of preservation, which (in terms of the health of library and archival collections) one might compare to the field of medicine. Indeed, the sense of the Hippocratic oath, to do no harm, certainly applies in both preservation and medicine. Although this bibliography is not an exhaustive one, it documents a preservation collection that will support any library's preservation program.

Readers are cautioned that Web site addresses often change. A negative search result may mean that a site no longer exists or merely that the URL has changed. In such cases, try a keyword search using a favorite search engine.

General Guidance

The Abbey Newsletter. [Online]. Provo, Utah: Abbey Publications, 1975– . Eight issues per year [cited 5 January 2001]. Available at <http://palimpsest.stanford.edu/byorg/abbey/>.

> This journal is available both online and in paper. Back issues are available in both formats, but as of early 2001, copyright restrictions prevented some articles from appearing online. The *Abbey Newsletter* includes pieces on all topics concerning preservation and conservation. The book review section is extensive, listing many publications and supplying lengthy critical reviews.

American Library Association. *Preservation Policy.* [Online]. Chicago: American Library Association, 30 June 1991 [cited 5 January 2001]. Available at <http://www.ala.org/alcts/publications/preservation.html>.

> ALA's preservation policy articulates the concept that preservation of information in all formats is necessary to enable every individual access to information. The policy states the aspiration of the Association to work "with standards-setting organizations to identify and develop

preservation standards and to promote compliance with those that already exist."

American Library Association. Library and Research Center. "Fact Sheet Number 1: How Many Libraries Are There in the United States?" [Online]. Chicago: American Library Association, 2001 [cited 5 January 2001]. Available at <http://www.ala.org/library/fact1.html>.

This sheet presents statistics on libraries in the United States, arranged by type.

Association of Research Libraries. Office of Management Studies. *Preservation Guidelines in ARL Libraries.* SPEC Kit 137. Washington, D.C.: Association of Research Libraries, Office of Management Studies, 1987.

This compilation of documents contains the ARL *Preservation Guidelines* and a reading list, as well as documents from sixteen ARL libraries that have preservation programs. Included are preservation policies, priority statements, suggestions for decision making, and descriptions of brittle books programs.

Banks, Paul N., and Roberta Pilette, eds. *Preservation: Issues and Planning.* Chicago: American Library Association, 2000.

This up-to-date volume deals with both traditional and current issues in preservation. It includes pieces on preservation programs for high-use libraries and archives, as well as exhibition policies and procedures, and information about the digitization and preservation of nonbook formats.

Carter, Robert. ". . . And What Do Librarians Want?" *Publishers Weekly* 237 (June 8, 1990): S12–S16.

This article reports the responses to the author's survey about the modern book publishing industry. In terms of librarians' complaints, poor book production was second only to inadequate discounts and was followed by spiraling prices.

Conservation OnLine (CoOL). *Resources for Conservation Professionals.* [Online] [cited 5 January 2001]. Available at <http://palimpsest.stanford.edu/>.

If a librarian is to bookmark only one preservation Web site, it must be this one, maintained by Stanford's expert and indefatigable Walter Henry. Here are search engines for locating preservation news and preservation people; preservation resources listed by author/organization/company; lists of archival suppliers; and directories of regional conservation centers, museums, historical societies, and libraries. A new area, "Conservation/Preservation Information for the General Public," fills a real gap. CoOL also links to many other preservation sites, including those of the Northern States Conservation Center (NSCC), the Northeast Document Conservation Center (NEDCC), and the

International Centre for the Study of the Preservation and Restoration of Cultural Property (ICCROM). Many organizations have placed their documents on the CoOL Web site. These include SOLINET, the Chicago Area Conservation Group (CACG), the Washington Conservation Guild, and the United Kingdom Institute for Conservation (UKIC). Technical documents run the gamut from NSCC's practical advice on pest control, security, and the environment to the Bishop Museum's collection aimed at the public and including articles such as "Bugs Are Eating My Family Treasures." Journals such as the *Alkaline Paper Advocate*, the *Abbey Newsletter,* and the *Journal of Conservation and Museum Studies* are also represented. CoOL contains the archives of the Conservation Distlist, also moderated by Walter Henry. This site is updated frequently.

Harris, Carolyn, Carol Mandel, and Robert Wolven. "A Cost Model for Preservation: The Columbia University Libraries' Approach." *Library Resources and Technical Services* 35 (January 1991): 33–54.

This article suggests how one might determine the price of preservation in any institution by providing a series of tables that analyze the costs associated with each activity. The tables include preservation tasks, the unit performing each activity, and all associated expenses—staff time, supervision, equipment, supplies, even the use of a bibliographic utility. These costs are then multiplied by the number of volumes in the collection to suggest the total expenditure for preservation operations.

Higginbotham, Barbra Buckner. *Our Past Preserved: A History of American Library Preservation, 1876–1910.* Boston: G. K. Hall, 1990.

This book is a historical account of the dawn of American library preservation, from the time of the founding of the American Library Association until the period just before the onset of the First World War. It covers the environment, binding, paper and ink, foreign influences, and the impact of preservation techniques for books on techniques for works of art on paper.

Higginbotham, Barbra Buckner, and Mary E. Jackson, eds. *Advances in Preservation and Access.* Vol. 1. Westport, Conn.: Meckler, 1992.

This collection of essays written by noted preservationists covers preservation policies, administrative agendas, options and opportunities, archival issues, and future challenges.

Higginbotham, Barbra Buckner, ed. *Advances in Preservation and Access.* Vol. 2. Medford, N.J.: Learned Information, 1995.

This compilation of twenty-five essays presents the preservation and conservation issues of primary interest to librarians and archivists in the mid-1990s. The volume is organized into seven sections: the future-present, science and technology, technology as a preservation tool, preservation planning (including condition surveys and needs assessments), special formats, special collections, and education and training.

Kyrillidou, Martha, Michael O'Connor, and Julia C. Blixrud, eds. and comps. *ARL Preservation Statistics 1996–97: A Compilation of Statistics from the Members of the Association of Research Libraries.* Washington, D.C.: Association of Research Libraries, 1998.

> Preservation statistics on staffing, expenditures, conservation treatment, and microfilming are covered for 115 of the 121 member libraries.

Lowry, Marcia D. *Preservation and Conservation in the Small Library.* Small Libraries Publications, no. 15. Chicago: Library Administration and Management Association, 1989.

> This pamphlet takes aim at the myth that preservation is an activity reserved for large research libraries. It explains how to determine what needs to be preserved and presents a range of preventative measures, including collection care, materials handling, and environmental controls. The author offers instructions on simple repairs that can be done in-house. She also advises on binding, caring for audiovisual materials, and planning for disasters. The book includes an appendix of purveyors of archival supplies.

Morrow, Carolyn Clark. "Developing Preservation Programs in Libraries." In *Issues in Library Management: A Reader for the Professional Librarian,* 97–127. White Plains, N.Y.: Knowledge Industry Pubs., 1984.

> This article begins with an illustrative needs analysis that shows how to determine what sort of preservation program is appropriate for any given library. Morrow demonstrates that preservation costs are easily defensible because they eliminate the need for recovery or replacement spending in the future. She illustrates that appropriate environmental and physical standards are major features of any preservation program and discusses ways in which damage by fire and flood can be minimized. The author suggests a range of conservation treatment options, concluding with a chart listing all the activities a preservation program might include, depending on library size and type.

Northeast Document Conservation Center. *Preservation of Library and Archival Materials: A Manual.* 3d ed., rev. and expanded. [Online]. Edited by Sherelyn Ogden. Andover, Mass.: Northeast Document Conservation Center, 1999 [cited 5 January 2001]. Available at <http://www.nedcc.org/plam3/newman.htm>.

> This invaluable manual is a collection of 49 leaflets previously issued both separately and in electronic format by the Northeast Document

Conservation Center. The pamphlets are arranged thematically under six topics: planning and prioritizing, the environment, emergency planning, storage and handling, reformatting, and conservation procedures. They consist of both instructions and lists of companies that provide the services described or stock the materials discussed. The leaflets are written in simple, easily understood terminology and can be used by beginners. Those that were issued earlier have been updated for this published manual, and new leaflets have been written to fill in any gaps, so that all the basic aspects of preservation are covered. The electronic versions of the leaflets appear on the NEDCC Web site, <http://www.nedcc.org/>, and are updated regularly. (Eleven of the leaflets are cited elsewhere in this bibliography.)

Ogden, Sherelyn. *Storage Furniture: A Brief Review of Current Options*. [Online]. Andover, Mass.: Northeast Document Conservation Center, 2000 [cited 5 January 2001]. Available at <http://www.nedcc.org/plam3/tleaf42.htm>.

Many of the materials from which shelving is made (including wood, wood composites, some sealants, adhesives, and baked enamels) contain chemicals that outgas or escape, eventually penetrating and damaging the items that bookcases and other furniture house. The author recommends the use of inert shelving materials and coatings, which act as a barrier between the shelf and the book. She describes the ways in which materials can be tested to ascertain whether they are leaching chemicals and provides contact information for professional testing services, home testing supplies, and furniture.

State Library of Ohio and the Ohio Preservation Council. *Managing Preservation: A Guidebook*. Columbus, Ohio: State Library, 1995.

This manual (written in nontechnical language) is a compilation of thirteen essays, each covering a different aspect of preservation. Among the topics included are conservation, binding, reformatting, and preservation funding.

Swartzburg, Susan G. *Preserving Library Materials: A Manual*. 2d ed. Metuchen, N.J.: Scarecrow, 1995.

Swartzburg presents the preservation basics: historical context, surveys of all types, collection management, environmental and physical considerations, emergency planning, bookbinding, reformatting, regional centers, standards, and the necessity for cooperation regionally, nationally, and internationally. The author goes into considerable detail on the care and preservation of nonbook materials, including photographs, motion pictures, sound recordings, and videotapes. Although not a how-to book, in its appendixes and bibliography the volume lists resources that fulfill that function. There is an extensive glossary, a comprehensive annotated list of preservation organizations, an annotated list of periodical publications, and a large annotated bibliography arranged by chapter. This volume is a must for any preservation library.

Bibliographies

Fox, Lisa L. *A Core Collection in Preservation.* 2d ed. Edited by Don K. Thompson and Joan ten Hoor. Chicago: Association for Library Collections and Technical Services; Atlanta: Southeastern Library Network, 1992.

> This annotated bibliography provides evaluative comments on books, films, and videos that deal with the preservation of both textual and nontextual materials.

Library and Archives Preservation: Selected Bibliography (SOLINET) [Online]. Atlanta: SOLINET, 2000 [cited 5 January 2001]. Available at <http://www.solinet.net/presvtn/leaf/presbib.htm>.

> This is a topically arranged bibliography with evaluative annotations. Ordering information is also provided.

The National Library of Australia. *Annotated Preservation Bibliography.* [Online]. Canberra, A.C.T.: National Library of Australia, n.d. [cited 5 January 2001]. Available at <http://www.nla.gov.au/chg/biblio.html>.

> This bibliography consists of ten pages of evaluative annotations for monographs as well as some discussion of serials, videos, and electronic publications.

Stuhr, Rebecca. *A Selective Preservation Bibliography.* [Online]. Grinnell, Iowa: Grinnel College Libraries, 2000 [cited 5 January 2001]. Available at <http://www.grinnell.edu/individuals/stuhrr/icpc/presbib99.html>.

> This bibliography is arranged by topic and format. Selected items are briefly annotated. Some preservation organizations are also included.

Binding

ABLE Library Binding Preparation Software. [Online]. Charlestown, Mass.: Acme Bookbinding, 2000 [cited 5 January 2001]. Available at <http://www.programmingconcepts.com/able/>.

> This program, available in Windows and on the Web, links the library's binding database with binders, facilitating the exchange of information and automating many of the activities associated with library binding.

Library Binding Institute. Library Binding Institute Standard for Library Binding. 8th ed. Rochester, N.Y.: Library Binding Institute, 1986.

This volume lays out and explains the Institute's standard for binding monographs and serials. Only binders who comply with the specifications set forth in this work can claim to perform according to the Library Binding Institute (LBI) standard. Certified library binders whose work is covered under the *Standard*'s warranty are listed by state, along with an illustrated glossary.

Merrill-Oldham, Jan, and Paul A. Parisi. *Guide to the Library Binding Institute Standard for Library Binding.* Chicago: American Library Association, 1990.

This guide is designed to be used in tandem with the *Standard for Library Binding* (1986). It explains the *Standard* in nontechnical language, enabling readers who are not part of the binding industry to use it to make decisions. The *Guide* also offers evaluative data that correspond to treatment options found in the *Standard*. It goes into more procedural detail, and its illustrations augment the *Standard*'s text.

Cleaning Collections

Ogden, Sherelyn. *Cleaning Books and Shelves.* [Online]. Andover, Mass.: Northeast Document Conservation Center, 2000 [cited 5 January 2001]. Available at <http://www.nedcc.org/plam3/tleaf43.htm>.

Cleanliness is critical to book preservation. Floors should be vacuumed regularly and mopped as need be. Ogden recommends using a magnetic wiping cloth to clean both books and shelves and explains proper technique. For very dusty books and shelves, a vacuum with a HEPA (High Efficiency Particulate) filter can be used. If shelves must be washed, it is essential that books never touch a wet surface. The author provides a list of suppliers for the products and implements discussed.

Ogden, Sherelyn. *Surface Cleaning of Paper.* [Online]. Andover, Mass.: Northeast Document Conservation Center, 2000 [cited 5 January 2001]. Available at <http://www.nedcc.org/plam3/tleaf62.htm>.

This leaflet outlines the process of cleaning paper without using liquids. It provides instructions for cleaning with a drafting brush, granules, a block eraser, and a vulcanized rubber sponge.

Watson, Joyce Frank. "Cleaning Collections." In *Moving Library Collections: A Management Handbook*, edited by Elizabeth Chamberlain Habich, 265–72. Westport, Conn.: Greenwood, 1998.

This essay points out the harm caused by the accumulation of dust on books and describes how to clean them using a vacuum (the preferred implement) or a treated dust cloth. It explains how to recognize and manage mold and insect infestations and provides several scenarios in which the cleaning of the collection can be incorporated with moving it.

The Collection Development Policy

American Library Association. Subcommittee on Guidelines for Collection Development. *Guide to the Evaluation of Library Collections*. Edited by Barbara Lockett. Collection Management and Development Guides, no. 2. Chicago: American Library Association, 1989. *See* annotation under "Preservation Planning."

American Library Association. Subcommittee to Revise the Guide for Written Collection Policy Statements. *Guide for Written Collection Policy Statements*. 2d ed. Edited by Joanne S. Anderson. Collection Management and Development Guides, no. 3. Chicago: Association for Library Collections and Technical Services, 1996.

> This guide provides the rationale for a written collection policy statement and describes how to formulate one for any library, regardless of its size or type. The *Guide* incorporates sample worksheets using the RLG and WLN conspectuses. Included are guidelines for making preservation policy decisions.

Evans, G. Edward, with Margaret R. Zarnosky. *Developing Library and Information Center Collections*. 4th ed. Library and Information Science Text Series. Englewood, Colo.: Libraries Unlimited, 2000.

> This text covers all phases of collection development, including "Protecting the Collection"; it is required reading in many collection development courses. This latest edition has a chapter on e-serials. To reduce the size of the book, information on the selection process and sample collection development policies were omitted from the text but can be found at <http://lib.lmu.edu/dlc4/> along with topical Webliographies, which are also found in the text.

Toward a New Vision for Reference: Kaleidoscope Collections and Reference Librarians. [Online] [cited 5 January 2001]. Available at <http://alexia.lis.uiuc.edu/~rrichard/RUSA/policies.html>.

> This Reference and User Services (RUSA) President's Program was held at the American Library Association's Annual Conference in June 1997. Included on this site are collection development bibliographies, articles, and sample policies that incorporate electronic materials.

Digitization

Brooklyn College Library Home Page. [Online] [cited 5 January 2001]. Available at <http://academic.brooklyn.cuny.edu/library/>.

> The Brooklyn College Library has a significant collection of Brooklyn-iana. A popular feature on the Web site is a series of virtual exhibits highlighting different aspects of these archival collections.

Conway, Paul. *Preservation in the Digital World*. [Online]. Washington, D.C.: Council on Library and Information Resources, 1996 [cited 5 January 2001]. Available at <http://www.clir.org/cpa/reports/conway2/>.

> The author places the preservation of digital objects in its historical context. He analyzes those parts of the process that are both in, and beyond, the librarian's control. Conway emphasizes the need for leadership so that cooperative ventures gain the required long-term commitments necessary to their survival. He includes a bibliography divided into four topics: preservation; digital preservation; microphotography; and technology, culture, and libraries.

Kenney, Anne R., and Oya Y. Rieger. *Moving Theory into Practice: Digital Imaging for Libraries and Archives*. Mountain View, Calif.: Research Libraries Group, 2000.

> This book presents the theoretical groundwork for making decisions about what to digitize, which method to elect, and the provisions that should be included in any contract for outsourcing. The authors suggest that decisions be based on the mission of each cultural institution. Each of the nine chapters includes sidebars that provide further detail on projects or issues mentioned in the body of the text. Although much technical information is included, the authors note that a technical manual can quickly become outdated: those contemplating digitalization projects should ensure that they are using the most recent data. This book's emphasis is critical thinking for complex decision making.

Knutson, Loes. "The Challenges of Preservation in a Digital Library Environment." *Current Studies in Librarianship* 22 (spring-fall 1998): 56–71.

> Knutson analyzes the philosophical issues surrounding the traditional roles of librarians in selecting, acquiring, organizing, providing access to, and preserving collections, plus the new skills required to perform these same activities in the digital environment. He notes that while digital information permits greater access than print formats, it is also inherently less stable. Knutson recommends international digitization standards and reviews the work of the Task Force on Archiving of Digital Information (1996) (described in this bibliography).

Research Libraries Group. "Preservation Working Group on Digital Archiving: Final Report: Recommendations for RLG." [Online]. 1998 [cited 5 January 2001]. Available at <http://www.rlg.org/preserv/archpre.html>.

> The RLG Preservation Working Group on Digital Archiving was formed to review the report "Preserving Digital Information," prepared by the Task Force on Archiving of Digital Information (*see* below). The Working Group recommends that RLG concentrate on three initiatives: identifying and analyzing the digital archiving needs of RLG member

institutions, examining and evaluating existing models for managing digital archiving facilities, and developing guidelines for appraisal, selection, and priority setting for preserving information in digital form. To meet the objectives of the first initiative, a survey was conducted and its findings issued in a report, "Digital Preservation Needs and Requirements in RLG Member Institutions," by Margaret Hedstrom and Sheon Montgomery (December 1998), which can be found at <http://www.rlg.org/preserv/digpres.html>.

Sitts, Maxine. *Handbook for Digital Projects: A Management Tool for Preservation and Access.* Andover, Mass.: Northeast Document Conservation Center, 2000.

> This collection of essays by notables in the field presents a thorough discussion of all aspects of digitization for preservation, as well as the preservation of the digitized materials themselves. Chapters cover the rationale for digitization, considerations for project management, and the selection of materials for scanning. The volume also includes an overview of copyright issues, technical considerations, case studies as guidelines for best practices, vendor relations, digital longevity, and an art historian's requirements for the use of and access to digital photographs.

Task Force on Archiving of Digital Information of the Commission on Preservation and Access and the Research Libraries Group. "Preserving Digital Information: Final Report and Recommendations." [Online]. 1996 [cited 5 January 2001]. Available at <http://www.rlg.org/ArchTF/>.

> This report describes the need for a national, systematic plan to preserve digital information. Among the recommendations detailed are the advancement of digital archives, the development of a national information structure to ensure the longevity of information, the coordination of digital preservation efforts, both nationally and internationally, and the identification of best practices in systems design. The Task Force emphasizes the centrality of migration to the maintenance of digital archives.

Emergency Planning

Brown, Karen E. *Worksheet for Outlining a Disaster Plan.* [Online]. Andover, Mass.: Northeast Document Conservation Center, 1999 [cited 5 January 2001]. Available at <http://www.nedcc.org/plam3/tleaf34.htm>.

> This is a complete checklist covering all items a library needs to address in the event of a disaster. Included are staffing, equipment, supplies, whom to call, and salvage priorities.

Fortson, Judith. *Disaster Planning and Recovery: A How-to-Do-It-Manual for Librarians and Archivists.* New York: Neal-Schuman, 1992.

> This manual explains how to develop a disaster preparedness plan. It

includes both prevention and recovery techniques for fire, water, wind, and earthquake damage; it also covers insurance. The author includes vendors and organizations that provide recovery services and a sample plan written for libraries in Oklahoma.

Kahn, Miriam B. *Disaster Response and Planning for Libraries.* Chicago: American Library Association, 1998.

This work provides the tools necessary to respond to various kinds of catastrophes, as well as those needed to avoid the problems that create disasters in the first place. The book details appropriate treatments for damaged materials in all formats and is arranged in four sections: response, recovery, prevention, and planning. Appendix A contains thirty checklists that address all aspects of recovery. Appendix B suggests sources for additional assistance and supplies.

National Fire Protection Association. *Guide for Fire Protection for Archives and Record Centers.* NFPA 232A. Quincy, Mass.: National Fire Protection Association, 1995.

This guide, which has undergone three revisions since it was issued in 1970, is intended to be used with the *Standard for the Protection of Records,* NFPA 232 (Quincy, Mass.: National Fire Protection Association, 2000), which does not contain provisions for protecting large archives and record centers. This document covers fire control, building construction, equipment, and facilities. It includes an appendix taken from Peter Waters's *Procedures for Salvage of Water-Damaged Library Materials* (*see* below), which is not part of the NFPA recommendations.

National Fire Protection Association. *Standard for the Protection of Cultural Resources Including Museums, Libraries, Places of Worship, and Historic Properties.* NFPA 909. Quincy, Mass.: National Fire Protection Association, 1997.

The National Fire Protection Association recognizes that older buildings pose special problems, as they cannot be retrofitted easily with fire alarm and sprinkler systems. The impetus for creating this standard was the number of catastrophic fires that occurred in the ten years before the publication of this book. The work provides guidelines that apply to a spectrum of structures, as well as specific guidelines for museums, libraries, places of worship, and historic properties. Included are specifications for fire precautions during alterations and renovations. The causes of fires that have occurred in major cultural institutions are discussed, as well as the associated costs.

New York State Program for the Conservation and Preservation of Library Research Materials. *Disaster Preparedness: Planning Resource Packet.* Albany: New York State Library, 1989.

This packet contains nine documents dealing with disaster prevention and salvage. Included is a guide to writing a disaster plan, which is still timely.

Trinkley, Michael. *Can You Stand the Heat? A Fire Safety Primer for Libraries, Archives, and Museums.* Atlanta: SOLINET, 1993.

> The author designs a fire safety program for cultural institutions. He emphasizes the importance of frequent inspections. Topics covered in this pamphlet are fire detection, alarm systems, sprinkler systems, manual fire extinguishing systems, and staff training.

Waters, Peter. *Procedures for Salvage of Water-Damaged Library Materials.* Washington, D.C.: Library of Congress, 1975.

> This is the standard work on flood recovery and has been incorporated into NFPA guidelines, cited above. It covers freezing, vacuuming, cleaning, washing, and interleaving water-damaged books, whether their injuries resulted from fire or flood. (Some of the recommended recovery techniques are now out-of-date, and some recommended chemicals are presently considered to be questionable.)

Environmental Controls

Environmental Controls Resource Packet. Albany: New York State Library, 1991.

> This packet contains four publications: *Conservation Environment Guidelines for Libraries and Archives,* by William P. Lull, with Paul N. Banks (Albany: State of New York, 1991; 87 p.), *Environmental Standards for Storage of Books and Manuscripts,* by Paul N. Banks (reprinted from *Library Journal* 99 [1974]: 339–43), *Environmental Specifications for the Storage of Library and Archival Materials* (Atlanta: SOLINET, 1985; 5 p.), and *Hold Everything! A Storage and Housing Information Sourcebook for Libraries and Archives by the New York Metropolitan Reference and Research Library Agency* (METRO) (New York: METRO, 1990; 63 p.). Together, these publications cover in great detail the effects on library materials of light (from all sources), temperature, pollution, and humidity. Instructions for measuring environmental factors and attaining the best conditions are included.

Gwinn, Nancy. "Politics and Practical Realities: Environmental Issues for the Library Administrator." In *Advances in Preservation and Access.* Vol. 1, edited by Barbra Buckner Higginbotham and Mary E. Jackson, 1351–46. Westport, Conn.: Meckler, 1992.

> The author places environmental problems in a historical context and reviews the literature. She makes suggestions about how to develop a rapprochement with building maintenance staff, developing in them a

greater appreciation of the often-conflicting issues of staff comfort and materials preservation. She advises setting realistic goals, creating preservation awareness among library staff, and apportioning preservation responsibilities among the different units in the library.

Lull, William P., with Paul N. Banks. *Conservation Environment Guidelines for Libraries and Archives.* Ottawa: Canadian Council of Archives, 1995.

This is an update of the earlier work found in the *Environmental Controls Resource Packet,* cited above. According to its preface, "This document discusses general collection environment criteria, criteria assessment, monitoring, and goals for an improved conservation environment." The authors present ideals as well as the compromises that new and renovated buildings often require.

Moving Collections

Habich, Elizabeth Chamberlain, ed. *Moving Library Collections: A Management Handbook.* Westport, Conn.: Greenwood, 1998.

This book deals with all aspects of moving a collection, with or without a moving company. Preserving the collection is considered in all stages of the moving process, in terms of cleaning, packing, transporting, shelving, and controlling pests.

White, Kris A. "Round 'Em Up, Move 'Em Out: How to Move and Preserve Archive Materials." *Conservation Administration News* 57 (April 1994): 16–17.

This article recounts the creative solutions employed to move the American Heritage Center's archival collection of fragile materials. White observes that it is crucial to budget adequately for archival-quality packing materials that *can* also serve as permanent containers.

Preservation Education

Boomgaarden, Wesley L., ed. *Staff Training and User Awareness in Preservation Management.* Preservation Planning Program Resources Guide Series. Washington, D.C.: Association of Research Libraries, 1993.

This guide gathers a wide range of policies, practices, guidelines, and promotional materials related to preservation education for both staff and readers. These materials take the form of memoranda, posters, bookmarks, and cartoons. The volume includes promotional material from ALA and a section on audiovisual aids for preservation education. It is aimed at an academic audience.

Drewes, Jeanne M., and Julie A. Page, eds. *Promoting Preservation Awareness in Libraries: A Sourcebook for Academic, Public, School, and Special*

Collections. Greenwood Library Management Collection. Westport, Conn.: Greenwood, 1997.

> The editors' thesis in this collection of essays is that a library preservation program must involve staff at every level and users of every age. The essayists demonstrate that preventative care involves the entire library community and requires a solid program of reader education. This volume presents theory, reinforced by case studies. It addresses the educational needs of library staff by function—catalogers, shelvers, reference staff, and so forth; it also covers both children and adult library users, as well as libraries of all types—academic, special, school, and public. Several successful strategies emerge: taking preservation to the target audience (by holding a book clinic in a location where undergraduates gather) and demonstrating to readers how to care for their personal collections (by offering workshops on the proper handling and storage of compact discs [CDs]).

Preservation Planning

American Library Association. Subcommittee on Guidelines for Collection Development. *Guide to the Evaluation of Library Collections.* Edited by Barbara Lockett. Collection Management and Development Guides, no. 2. Chicago: American Library Association, 1989.

> This guide lists methods of evaluating a library collection. For each, it cites both the advantages and disadvantages. Tools include checklists, comparative statistics, collection standards, circulation statistics, in-house usage data, user opinion surveys, shelf availability studies, interlibrary loan statistics, citation studies, and document delivery tests.

Banks, Paul N., and Roberta Pilette, eds. *Preservation: Issues and Planning.* Chicago: American Library Association, 2000. *See* annotation under "General Guidance."

Calipr: Preservation Planning Software. [Online]. Berkeley: California State Library, 1999 [cited 5 January 2001]. Available at <http://sunsite.berkeley.edu/CALIPR/>.

> Calipr (California Preservation) is a software package and manual developed at the University of California at Berkeley Library. This product gives the neophyte the tools to conduct a condition survey and use the results to make decisions about preservation priorities. It poses thirteen questions whose answers can suggest as many as nine different preservation actions. Using Calipr is like having a preservation expert perched on one's shoulder, demonstrating how to sample, asking the relevant questions, and leading the librarian to the appropriate solutions based on his or her responses. The package is designed to be used either to develop an institutional preservation plan or to derive data to support a

cooperative venture. Calipr is intended to be a starting point leading to further reading in the literature before a plan is formulated.

Darling, Pamela W., and Duane E. Webster, comps. *Preservation Planning Program: An Assisted Self-Study Manual for Libraries.* Rev. ed. Revised by Jan Merrill-Oldham and Jutta Reed-Scott. Washington, D.C.: Association of Research Libraries, 1993.

> This revision of the 1987 work explains how to assess preservation needs, set priorities, and plan a program with the participation of the library staff. Areas covered include environmental control, the physical condition of the collection, organization of preservation units, disaster preparedness, and staff and user education.

Ogden, Sherelyn. *The Needs Assessment Survey.* [Online]. Andover, Mass.: Northeast Document Conservation Center, 1999 [cited 5 January 2001]. Available at <http://www.nedcc.org/plam3/tleaf13.htm>.

> This leaflet discusses the elements that comprise a needs assessment survey. It also contrasts the advantages and disadvantages of choosing an outside surveyor or using in-house staff.

Ogden, Sherelyn. *Preservation Planning: Guidelines for Writing a Long-Range Plan.* Professional Practice Series. Washington, D.C.: American Association of Museums; Andover, Mass.: Northeast Document Conservation Center, 1997.

> This spiral-bound workbook, designed for the novice, offers step-by-step instructions on how to formulate a preservation plan. It also provides assistance in creating the collection survey, which precedes the development of any plan. Appendix 7 is a sample plan with work sheets. This volume gives the reader the tools necessary to prioritize preservation needs and to devise realistic timetables for executing the tasks included in the preservation plan. Blank work sheets are included in the workbook as well as on a disk.

Promotional Material: General

Bookmarks and Bookbags. [Online]. La Jolla: University of California at San Diego, n.d. [cited 5 January 2001]. Available at <http://gort.ucsd.edu/preseduc/bookmark.htm>.

> This site provides links to displays of bookmarks and posters from Indiana University and New York University and guidelines on making one's own graphics.

SOLINET Resources for Preservation Staff and User Education. [Online]. Atlanta: SOLINET, 2000 [cited 5 January 2001]. Available at <http://www.solinet.net/presvtn/leaf/presed.htm>.

> The site describes books, videos, and graphic materials from a number

of sources, including the American Library Association, the British Library, the Canadian Council on Archives, Demco, Indiana University, and the Library of Congress.

Promotional Material: Videos

Preservation videos can be used for educating staff or for creating reader awareness. Often they dramatize the negative consequences of ignoring preservation needs and provide instruction in simple preservation methods.

Basic Book Repair with Jane Greenfield. 30 min. Wilson, 1988. Videocassette.

Greenfield, conservator at Yale University, demonstrates how to repair a torn page, a cut page, a broken hinge, a shaken hinge, and a flapping spine. All tools and materials are explained and listed in the accompanying guide. To make maximum use of this video, it is helpful to draw upon the text of Greenfield's illustrated work *Books: Their Care and Repair,* also described in this bibliography (*see* below).

How to Operate a Book. 30 min. Book Arts Press, School of Library Service, Columbia University, 1986. Videocassette.

Set in the rare book collection at the Firestone Library, Princeton University, this video explores the history of book structures, concentrating on developments that have occurred since the advent of the codex. Reformatting through microfilming and photocopying is also examined. Instructions on the proper care of rare books using cushioning pads and polyethylene reading cradles are illustrated.

Into the Future: On the Preservation of Knowledge in the Electronic Age. 30 min. and 60 min. American Film Foundation and Sanders & Mock Productions, in association with the Commission on Preservation and Access and American Council of Learned Societies, 1997. Videocassette.

The problem of preserving the digital record is examined. The documentary stresses the need to migrate digital data to new platforms and formats and to identify new ways of preserving electronic information.

Let Us Save What Remains. 15 min. Virginia State Library and Archives, 1991. Videocassette.

This video presents an assortment of historically significant maps, letters, photographs, and documents that are displayed while the narrator reads excerpts from them. Items that are damaged beyond repair are also shown. The video illustrates that much destruction can be prevented through humidity and temperature control, proper handling and shelving, encasing important items in mylar, and safeguarding the intellectual content of works by duplicating them. Examples are tailored for Virginia to encourage participation in a grants program for the preservation of state records. This video could be adapted for use in other locations.

Library Binding: A Shared Responsibility, A Collaborative Effort. 26 min.
Library of Congress, National Preservation Program, 1990. Videocassette.

> This video examines the causes of damage to bindings, illustrates
> binding procedures, and promotes good communication between the
> bindery and the library staff.

Milevski, Robert. J. *Books in General Collections: Paper Repair and Pockets.*
81 min. Library of Congress, National Preservation Program, 1987.
Videocassette.

> This video provides step-by-step instructions on how to repair paper and
> pockets in books. It was filmed at a conference sponsored by ALA and
> the National Preservation Program Office at the Library of Congress,
> August 26–30, 1985.

Murder in the Stacks. 15 min. Preservation Department, Columbia
University, 1987. Videocassette.

> This video uses actors to portray Sherlock Holmes and Dr. Watson, who
> discover that library books are "murdered" by staff and readers who
> shelve and handle them improperly.

Providing a Future for the Past. 13 min. UMI Preservation Division, 1990.
Videocassette.

> In this video notable librarians discuss the problem of brittle books and
> demonstrate the preservation microfilming service performed at
> University Microfilms (now Bell and Howell Information and
> Learning).

*Safeguarding Our Cultural Heritage: Highlights from the National Summit on
Emergency Response.* 37 min. Getty Conservation Institute, 1995.
Videocassette.

> This video presents excerpts from the National Summit on Emergency
> Response, which took place December 1, 1994, and was sponsored by
> the Federal Emergency Management Agency (FEMA), the Getty
> Conservation Institute, and the National Institute for the Conservation
> of Cultural Property. More than eighty organizations were represented.
> A coordinated response to natural disasters is needed with efforts to
> protect collections as well as the buildings that house them. The
> speeches focus on anticipating emergencies in order to prevent loss and
> speed recovery.

Slow Fires: On the Preservation of the Human Record. 33 min. American Film
Foundation, 1987. Videocassette.

> Focusing on the problem of acidic paper, the video illustrates the causes
> of deterioration in library and archival materials.

These Web sites list videos available for loan or purchase:

Amigos Library Services: <http://www.amigos.org/preservation/illvideo.html>

Pennsylvania Preservation Consortium: <http://www.papres.org/info2-3.html>

SOLINET: <http://www.solinet.net/presvtn/leaf/presed.htm>

University of California, San Diego: <http://gort.ucsd.edu/preseduc/video.htm>

Public Libraries

Tolbert, Susan L. "Preservation in American Public Libraries: A Contradiction in Terms?" *Public Libraries* 36 (July-August 1997): 236–45.

> The author sets out to dispel the belief that preservation is strictly the purview of the research library. She discusses the full range of preservation activities and shows how these activities, both preventative and curative, can save the public library from sustaining heavy losses caused by the improper handling of heavily used materials, poor storage, inadequate buildings, and disasters, natural or otherwise. A series of helpful tables includes preservation activities appropriate to public libraries, tips for disaster mitigation, and useful supplies.

Reformatting

Dalton, Steve. Microfilm and Microfiche. [Online]. Andover, Mass.: Northeast Document Conservation Center, 1999 [cited 5 January 2001]. Available at <http://www.nedcc.org/plam3/tleaf51.htm>.

> This NEDCC leaflet points out the advantages of microfilming over digitization (under optimal circumstances, microfilm can last five hundred years and does not require sophisticated equipment to read; digital media have much shorter life spans and require an ever-changing array of complex access equipment). Microfilming quality control by both vendor and consumer are also covered. The author presents recommendations for microform storage environments, enclosures, handling, equipment, disaster preparedness, and vendor selection. He offers guidelines for creating master, duplicate negative, and service copies.

Fox, Lisa L, ed. *Preservation Microfilming: A Guide for Librarians and Archivists.* 2d ed. Chicago: American Library Association, 1996.

> This manual covers all aspects of preservation microfilming, including administration, selection, materials preparation, standards, practices, bibliographic control, and costs. This edition "reflects technical advances" that have occurred since the first edition (edited by Nancy Gwinn) and the "growth and diversity of cooperative microfilming projects."

National Endowment for the Humanities. *United States Newspaper Program.* [Online]. Washington, D.C.: National Endowment for the Humanities, n.d. [cited 5 January 2001]. Available at <http://www.neh.gov/preservation/usnp.html>.

See annotation under "Special Formats: Newspapers."

Resources for Facsimile Replacement of Out-of-Print and Brittle Books. [Online]. Andover, Mass.: Northeast Document Conservation Center, 2000 [cited 5 January 2001]. Available at <http://www.nedcc.org/plam3/tleaf52.htm>.

This leaflet furnishes the contact information for six companies that make facsimile replacements.

Repair

Greenfield, Jane. *Books: Their Care and Repair.* New York: Wilson, 1983.

This manual, illustrated with simple line drawings, instructs the reader in how to make simple repairs. A glossary, general information on book structure, the causes of deterioration, and exhibition techniques are also included.

Horton, Richard. *Protecting Books with Custom-Fitted Boxes.* [Online]. Andover, Mass.: Northeast Document Conservation Center, 2000 [cited 5 January 2001]. Available at <http://www.nedcc.org/plam3/tleaf45.htm>.

This leaflet describes the conditions that make it advisable to enclose books in boxes. Included are systematic directions for building enclosures, accompanied by illustrations for measuring books for custom-made boxes and a list of companies that make them to order.

Milevski, Robert J. *Book Repair Manual.* Carbondale: Illinois Cooperative Conservation Program, 1984.

This heavily illustrated manual is the outgrowth of a series of workshops given by the author. It encompasses detailed instructions for making four simple repairs: tightening hinges and replacing endsheets, recasing the textblock, replacing a worn spine, and tipping pages into bound volumes. The tools and supplies needed to make each repair are included, along with suppliers and (1984) prices.

Milevski, Robert J., and Linda Nainis. "Implementing a Book Repair and Treatment Program." *Library Resources and Technical Services* 31 (April 1987): 159–76.

This article covers the steps involved in setting up a book repair and treatment program. It is organized into four parts: justification, space and equipment, personnel, and selection. It is not a "hands-on piece" and does not include instructions on how to make repairs. Instead, that information can be found in Milevski's *Book Repair Manual* (above).

Ogden, Sherelyn. *Encapsulation in Polyester Film Using Double-Sided Tape.* [Online]. Andover, Mass.: Northeast Document Conservation Center,

2000 [cited 5 January 2001]. Available at <http://www.nedcc.org/plam3/tleaf65.htm>.

> This illustrated leaflet gives systematic instructions on how to encapsulate a document. Included are the names and addresses of companies that stock the required materials to do this work.

Ogden, Sherelyn. *Repairing Paper Artifacts*. [Online]. Andover, Mass.: Northeast Document Conservation Center, 2000 [cited 5 January 2001]. Available at <http://www.nedcc.org/plam3/tleaf63.htm>.

> This leaflet provides instructions for making simple repairs. It gives detailed advice on preferred papers, adhesive ingredients, and adhesive formulas. Included is a list of suppliers for all the materials discussed.

Paris, Jan. *Choosing and Working with a Conservator*. [Online]. 1990. Reprint, with new information, Andover, Mass.: Northeast Document Conservation Center, 1999 [cited 5 January 2001]. Available at <http://www.nedcc.org/plam3/tleaf69.htm>.

> Paris explains in general terms what a conservator does, what qualifications he or she should have, and how to locate a conservator. She lists the questions one should pose, those the conservator should ask in turn, and questions for the prospective conservator's references. She touches on the way costs are determined and what to look for when any job is finished. Paris explains some of the qualities a work that has been properly conserved should embody. The article is followed by an annotated bibliography and lists of information resources, conservation training programs, and regional conservation centers. The organizations listed can assist with locating a qualified conservator and with implementing a collection survey, should that be warranted.

Security

Association of College and Research Libraries. "Guidelines for the Security of Rare Books, Manuscripts, and Other Special Collections." [Online]. Chicago: Association of College and Research Libraries, 1999 [cited 5 January 2001]. Available at <http://www.ala.org/acrl/guides/raresecu.html>.

> This report presents guidelines aiding cultural institutions in safeguarding valuable materials. Recommendations include choosing a security administrator who will show restraint in giving out keys, change locks when employees leave, exercise care about those hired to work with special materials, secure the library or archive at the close of each day, and provide lockers so that researchers are unencumbered by coats, book bags, or notebooks. This booklet also includes guidelines for marking special materials.

Special Formats

General Works

Henderson, Kathryn Luther, and William T. Henderson, eds. *Conserving and Preserving Materials in Nonbook Formats*. Urbana-Champaign: University of Illinois, Graduate School of Library and Information Science, 1991.

This book is a collection of papers presented at the thirtieth Allerton Park Institute, November 6–9, 1988. Topics include sound recordings, computer files, motion pictures, newspapers, photographs, textiles, cartographic materials, and preservation planning.

Swartzburg, Susan Garretson., ed. *Conservation in the Library: A Handbook of Use and Care of Traditional and Nontraditional Materials*. Westport, Conn.: Greenwood, 1983.

This collection of essays concentrates primarily on the care of nonbook materials, with chapters on photographs, slides, microforms, film, videotape, sound recordings, and videodiscs.

Archival Collections

Ritzenthaler, Mary Lynn. *Preserving Archives and Manuscripts*. Archival Fundamental Series. Chicago: Society of American Archivists, 1993.

This illustrated guide is a thorough treatment of the preservation of archives and manuscripts. The author advocates the integration of preservation into all archival functions. The appendixes include an extensive bibliography and a twenty-eight page manual (enhanced by line drawings) providing instructions on basic preservation procedures.

Cartographic Materials

Larsgaard, Mary Lynette. *Map Librarianship: An Introduction*. 3d ed. Englewood, Colo.: Libraries Unlimited, 1998.

This volume covers the selection and acquisitions; cataloging and classification; storage, care, and repair; and preservation of cartographic materials in both traditional and modern formats, including maps, globes, atlases, remote sensing images, relief models, and electronic forms. The author describes the special qualities of spatial data, which have particular cataloging, storage, and handling needs.

Music

Gertz, Janet E., with Susan Blaine. "Preservation of Printed Music: The Columbia University Libraries Scores Condition Survey." *Fontes Artis Musicae* 41 (July/September 1994): 261–69.

A Columbia University condition survey found a substantial number of music scores printed on acidic paper; some of these were recently published. Given the special uses of scores (*see* Sommer's article, below), reformatting is not a desirable preservation option. Thus, scores should be printed on alkaline paper, bound appropriately, and housed in locations where recognized standards for temperature and humidity control are enforced.

Sommer, Susan T. "Knowing the Score: Preserving Collections of Music." *Fontes Artis Musicae* 41 (July/September 1994): 256–60.

This paper was originally presented at a program of the same name jointly sponsored by the Music Library Association and ALA's Association for Library Collections and Technical Services, Preservation of Library Materials Section, held during the 1991 Annual Conference of ALA, in Atlanta, Georgia. It addresses the special problems encountered in reformatting and protecting music material.

Newspapers

Library of Congress. *Preserving Newspapers*. [Online]. Washington, D.C.: Library of Congress, 2000 [cited 5 January 2001]. Available at <http://lcweb.loc.gov/preserv/care/newspap.html>.

This report discusses how to care for, store, and handle newspapers, as well as the different methods of preserving the information that they contain. It also covers digitization of microfilm copies.

Library of Congress. *United States Newspaper Program*. [Online]. Washington, D.C.: Library of Congress, 2000 [cited 5 January 2001]. Available at <http://lcweb.loc.gov/preserv/usnppr.html>.

This paper gives the history of the U.S. Newspaper Program. It explains the value of newspapers to historians and the preservation issues that arise in dealing with this medium. It also includes a bibliography.

National Endowment for the Humanities. *United States Newspaper Program*. [Online]. Washington, D.C.: National Endowment for the Humanities, n.d. [cited 5 January 2001]. Available at <http://www.neh.gov/preservation/usnp.html>.

This document describes a project funded by NEH that promotes and supports the cataloging and preservation of newspapers on microfilm. The site includes a state-by-state list of the titles cataloged and microfilmed, as well as those housed in eight national repositories and the Library of Congress. Contact information for state project directors and the national repository are included, plus the Web sites for each state's project.

Objects

National Park Service. *Conserve-O-Gram Series.* [Online]. Washington, D.C.: National Park Service, 2000 [cited 5 January 2001]. Available at <http://www.cr.nps.gov/csd/publications/conserveogram/cons_toc.html>.

This Web site has more than one hundred documents, called conserve-o-grams, prepared between 1993 and the present. They cover the "preventative conservation" of all sorts of museum objects. The material is also available in loose-leaf format.

Photographs

Roosa, Mark. *Care, Handling, and Storage of Photographs.* [Online]. Washington, D.C.: Library of Congress, Preservation Directorate, 1992 [cited 5 January 2001]. Available at <http://www.lcweb.loc.gov/preserv/care/photolea.html>.

This paper amply demonstrates just how delicate photographs are. It provides a history of photographic processes, on the premise that it is necessary to know the process in order to care properly for the items. Roosa delves into environmental factors, housekeeping, storage, enclosures, and handling for the various types and sizes of photographs. A bibliography, standards, and a list of suppliers are also included.

Plastics

Williams, Scott R., and Tom Edmondson. "Know Your Plastics: Safe Enclosures for Book and Nonbook Materials." Paper presented at the annual meeting of the American Library Association at a joint session of the ALCTS Preservation and Reformatting Section and the American Institute for the Conservation of Historic and Artistic Works, Chicago, July 2000. (Available on cassette from ALA.)

Williams, a chemist, and Edmondson, a photographic conservator, made presentations at this program in which they explained the chemical makeup of the plastics often found in library collections and in enclosures intended to protect collections. They illustrate the degradation process of some plastics and show how this process can negatively affect the item enclosed as well as adjacent material.

Scrapbooks

Zucker, Barbara Fleisher. *Preservation of Scrapbooks and Albums.* [Online]. Washington, D.C.: Library of Congress, Preservation Directorate, 1998 [cited 5 January 2001]. Available at <http://www.lcweb.loc.gov/preserv/care/scrapbk.html>.

Scrapbooks and albums are difficult to preserve, and they often come to the library damaged in some way. Because of the various items they house, scrapbooks are difficult to store and maintain. This article presents guidelines for making decisions about collection policy, the environment, storage, handling, treatment, and reformatting. The author provides information about companies that sell the materials discussed in this article.

Sound Recordings

Kodak Digital Science Solutions. *Permanence, Care, and Handling of CDs.* [Online] [cited 5 January 2001]. Available at <http://www.kodak.com/US/en/digital/techInfo/permanence.shtml>.

This series of ten leaflets thoroughly explains all aspects of the longevity, care, and handling of all types of audio materials and CD-ROMs. Topics covered include CD types, life expectancy, safe handling, storage, and permanence (including migration and storage in multiple formats in different locations).

Textiles

Henry Ford Museum and Greenfield Village. *The Care and Preservation of Antique Textiles and Costumes.* [Online]. Dearborn, Mich.: Henry Ford Museum and Greenfield Village, n.d. [cited 5 January 2001]. Available at <http://www.hfmgv.org/histories/cis/textile.html>.

This paper presents guidelines for the care of valuable textiles in museums or at home. Natural fibers will disintegrate owing to the actions of light, pests, heat, and humidity. Environmental monitoring, proper storage, and good housekeeping are essential to the preservation of these materials. The ideal way to store costumes is flat; rugs are best rolled; and small items keep well when they are framed.

Web Sites

Casey, Carol. "The Cyberarchive: A Look at the Storage and Preservation of Web Sites." *College and Research Libraries* 59 (July 1998): 304–10.

Casey addresses the problem of the disappearing Web site. She details reasons why Web sites are not yet treated with the same reverence as other forms of the human record and briefly touches on both the means of determining which Web sites should be preserved and on the mechanics of creating an electronic archive.

Works of Art on Paper

Henry Ford Museum and Greenfield Village. *The Care and Preservation of Works of Art on Paper.* [Online]. Dearborn, Mich.: Henry Ford Museum and Greenfield Village, n.d. [cited 5 January 2001]. Available at <http://www.hfmgv.org/histories/cis/paper.html>.

This document discusses the characteristics of paper and the preservation requirements of the many media used to create art on paper. It outlines the elements that cause artwork to deteriorate and instructs on proper handling, environment, storage, cleaning, and conservation. The document draws attention to the particular fragility of some agents, such as watercolors, which will fade if exposed to much light, and pastel and charcoal, which can separate from paper if not stored properly in window mats or individual boxes.

Standards

AIIM International. *Association for Information and Image Management Standards Program.* [Online]. Silver Spring, Md.: AIIM International, n.d. [cited 5 January 2001]. Available at <http://www.aiim.org/standards.cfm>.

This association is an accredited American National Standards Institute development organization. The Association for Information and Image Management Standards (AIIM) is centrally involved in the development and dissemination of standards for microforms and other imaging systems. Their standards and technical reports are available for purchase via the Web.

Library of Congress. *Standards.* [Online]. Washington, D.C.: Library of Congress, 2000 [cited 5 January 2001]. Available at <http://lcweb.loc.gov/standards/standard.html>.

LC maintains the following standards used in the exchange of information: MARC (Machine Readable Cataloging) formats, which are standards for bibliographic information; Z39.50, an information retrieval protocol for communicating between different systems; ISO Language Code 639-2, which represents language names; Encoded Archival Description (EAD), a Standardized Generalized Markup Language (SGML) for finding aids to collections of material; and digital library standards for LC's digital library projects. Related national and international standards are also linked to this site.

National Information Standards Organization. 4733 Bethesda Ave., Ste. 300, Bethesda, MD 20814. (301) 654-2512. E-mail: nisohq@niso.org. <http://www.niso.org/>

The National Information Standards Organization (NISO) is accredited as a standards developer by the American National Standards Institute, the national clearinghouse for U.S. standards development. It develops and promotes voluntary technical standards for the information industry. NISO has developed more than thirty standards, of which the following are examples: Z39.50 (for information retrieval), 12083 (a Standard Generalized Markup Language [SGML] tool), Z39.2 (Information Interchange Format), Z39.18 (Scientific and Technical Reports), and codes for languages and countries. Using standards facilitates compatibility among data, equipment, and practices used by libraries and publishers. All NISO standards are available gratis on their Web site. They represent the United States at the International Organization for Standardization (ISO).

See also the RLG Preservation Program (PRESERV), <http://www.rlg.org/ preserv/>, in this resource guide.

Index

Since 1985 **Barbra Buckner Higginbotham** has been the director of the Brooklyn College Library of the City University of New York, where she also teaches in the English department. In fall 1994 she assumed the additional responsibility of academic computing and the title Executive Director of Academic Information Technologies. Before coming to Brooklyn, Higginbotham served for eight years in the Columbia University Libraries; she also taught in Columbia's School of Library Service. She holds an undergraduate degree in English literature from Centenary College of Louisiana, and a master's and a doctorate in library science from Columbia University.

Higginbotham's research interests include preservation and technology, and she writes and lectures in both fields. Her most recent books include volume two of *Advances in Preservation and Access* (Learned Information, 1995); *Access versus Assets: A Comprehensive Resource Sharing Manual for Academic Librarians* (ALA, 1993); *Advances in Preservation and Access* (Meckler, 1992); and *Our Past Preserved: A History of American Library Preservation, 1875-1910* (G. K. Hall, 1990).

A past-president of the Library and Information Technology Association, a division of the American Library Association, Higginbotham is currently the project director for two large federal grants that support Web-based teaching.

Judith W. Wild is head of Technical Services at the Brooklyn College Library, the City University of New York, where she has worked since 1981. She serves on the Library Cabinet, or policy-making body. During her tenure at Brooklyn, she has also taught at the Queens College and Pratt Institute Graduate Library Schools. She earned a bachelor's degree from Brooklyn College, a master's degree and a specialist degree in educational technology from Indiana University, and a master's in library science from Columbia University.

Wild learned firsthand about disaster recovery in 1992, when the Brooklyn College Library suffered two floods. She worked closely with the preservation consultant then and subsequently, when the library received a gift of rare Ethiopian materials. Before assuming her post at Brooklyn College, she held technical services positions at the Parliamentary Library, Canberra, Australia, and at the National Library of Australia, also in Canberra. She has published in library journals and has cochaired the LITA/ALCTS Retrospective Conversion Interest Group and chaired the LITA/OCLC Frederick G. Kilgour Award Committee for Research in Library and Information Technology.